The *Glasgow Herald* Book of Club Golf

THE GLASGOW HERALD BOOK OF
CLUB GOLF

DOUGLAS LOWE

MAINSTREAM
PUBLISHING

IN CONJUNCTION WITH

First published in Great Britain in 1990 by
MAINSTREAM PUBLISHING COMPANY (EDINBURGH) LTD
in conjunction with the *GLASGOW HERALD*
7 Albany Street
Edinburgh EH1 3UG

British Library Cataloguing in Publication Data

Lowe, Douglas
  Glasgow Herald Book of Golf
  1. Scotland. Golf, history
  I. Title
  796.35209411

  ISBN 1 85158 386 6

Typeset in 11/13 Garamond in Great Britain by Beecee Typesetting Services
Printed in Great Britain by Dotesios Printers Ltd., Trowbridge

CONTENTS

PREFACE
9

FOREWORD
by Raymond Jacobs
11

TAKE A TIP
13

PARLIAMO GOWF
88

A CHANCE IN TEN BILLION
97

SPOILED FOR CHOICE
111

IN SEARCH OF A CHAMPION
129

A DEGREE OF HELP
134

WHO IS THE GODFATHER?
143

A TOUCH OF THE BIZARRE
161

SINISTER LINKS WITH SHINTY
168

ON THE DISTAFF SIDE
171

THE POWER OF PERSONALITY
182

THE EQUALISING FACTORS
198

THE BMW SYNDROME
203

ACKNOWLEDGMENTS

Thanks are due to Wm Teacher & Sons for subsidising this book thereby enabling the cover price to be kept below £5, to Val Graham, the *Herald*'s Publicity and Promotions Manager, to Robert Tweedie of the *Herald* Picture Library, and to freelance journalist Elspeth Burnside, who took over collection of the golf tips in mid-1989. Percy Huggins has kindly allowed the reprinting of the article on my favourite nine holes, first published in *Golf World Scotland* and the material on golf scholarship has been reprinted with the permission of the *Scottish Golfer*, newspaper of the Scottish Golf Union. Tom Shields has permitted the reprinting of his article 'Deck of Cards' from *Bogeys — The Really Serious Golf Comic*. In a project like *Club Golf*, various departments are involved and valuable assistance is further acknowledged from colleagues on the sports desk, picture desk, computer systems, cuttings library, caseroom and copytakers. The pictures used in this book are the work of *Glasgow Herald* staff photographers James Galloway, Duncan Dingsdale, Stuart Paterson, Edward Jones, James Millar, Arthur Kinloch, Ian Hossack, and Angela Catlin, and freelances Don Robertson, Brian Logue, Randolph Caughie, Donald Wren and Walter Kerr.

Perhaps the most important contribution is from golf club match secretaries who have the task of sending in their competition results and other information without which there would have been no Club Golf Tuesday page and no book.

A turn for the better — George MacKay gives Douglas Lowe a hint on how to get things right

PREFACE

In the beginning there were Club Golf returns. Ever since the earliest days a golfer who had put in a good score wanted the world to know about it even if no one else was the slightest bit interested. Indeed, it has often been said that a golfer listens to other golfers' stories only because in return he will have a chance to tell his, rather in the same vein, as travellers' tales. So it has been that fine clubs like Glasgow and Prestwick and the ladies of Troon and Belleisle have sent in details of their competition winners for just about as long as they have existed. A former Sports Editor of the *Glasgow Herald* once made the mistake of deciding they were unimportant and stopped publishing them. Such was the outcry that the policy lasted only a few weeks. Club Golf had proved to be immovable.

Even as recently as the beginning of 1988 they were regarded by staff on the sports desk as a nuisance. Stronger words were on occasion used by the poor soul who was landed with editing them after the pile, especially in summer, had built itself up into a paper mountain. They were published erratically, usually to fill up space on a quiet day. And if, at five minutes to edition time, there was an unexpected gap on a sports page, the cry would be: 'Dig out the Club Golf returns'. In this respect they were sometimes useful, even if they were generally a problem.

Like many significant changes in the history of the world, the turnaround came as a result of a lunch, a fairly longish one as far as I have been able to make out, the participants being Sports Editor Eddie Rodger (Haggs Castle) and Editor Arnold Kemp (unattached). The idea was to turn a problem into a virtue. So it came to pass that, being one of the nuttier golfers on the sports desk, I was asked to produce a weekly Club Golf page every Tuesday, beginning May 1988.

The ideas flowed from that point. The then Publicity and Promotions Manager, Bill Soutar (Bonnyton), suggested a golf tip from a different club professional each week, and the brainwave of sifting out the best scores from returns and tabulating them was rounded off by Chief Sub-editor Guy Murphy (Cawder) who came up with the name 'Parbusters'. Further wheezes were chipped in by colleagues — golf correspondent Raymond Jacobs (Glasgow and Royal and Ancient), Jim Reynolds (Mount Ellen) and Doug Gillon (Hilton Park). The project was on the first tee.

Wm Teacher & Sons joined the fray in 1989 by giving bottles of Teacher's Highland Cream to weekly section winners while the *Glasgow Herald* put up prizes of golf balls, the effort culminating in October 1989 at Haggs Castle with the first Parbusters Final. The Club Golf page had finally moved out of the office and on to the course.

The book makes no attempt at being comprehensive; it is more of a miscellany of the material collected in the first two years. It predominantly covers the west of the traditional *Glasgow Herald* circulation area but, in line with the newspaper's policy, we are continuing to aim nationally and hope that participating clubs in the north and east, of which there are a small but growing number, will continue to increase. You can become involved by sending your competition results and news on our free Linkline number 0800 833333, details of which are at the end of the book.

The project has the support of the Scottish Golf Union and the Council of National Golf Unions, representatives of whom are monitoring results especially to find out whether the variable standard scratch-score system is working. Initial indications are that it is, not least because the 'bandits' identified in our columns are, in reality, nothing of the kind, their scores having been statistically justified as what would be expected from a field of around 10,000, which is what our weekly results service represents.

What follows is the outcome of the first two years.

FOREWORD

by R a y m o n d   J a c o b s
Golf Correspondent of the *Glasgow Herald*

The dedication of this foreword is unequivocal. It is to that band of brothers — those unrepentantly beguiled legions — who try not to let their reach exceed their grasp, but will insist, against all experience and common sense, on taking the No. 7 iron instead of the No. 5; who relish being among the Militant Tendency of the Dirty Bar to indulge the prerogative of oppositions through the ages, having the solution to everything with the responsibility for nothing; who seek endlessly for improvement and are usually denied it, except just often enough to be convinced that their shortcomings are aberrations, not the regular flaws they really are.

Golf being the game it is, club golfers are endlessly seduced into that innocent self-deception which believes the lie, that they are not the hot shots they think they are, which, of course, their fellow-players, sometimes by observation and as frequently by loss of earnings, have always known to be true. The trouble is that those same critics are just as badly at fault as the objects of their scepticism. The fraternity of the game is, therefore, something of an unholy alliance, in which absence of total anarch is preserved only by a mutual recognition, not infrequently a little shaky in the observance however well-meaning in the breach, of the etiquette and the rules which govern the essential civilities and conduct of the game.

The club golfer does not look for perfection; even the most tunnel-visioned seekers after wisdom and truth know that for them it cannot exist. They are not about to dismantle and reconstruct their swings, like latter-day Nick Faldos. All they want to know is how to develop a reasonably dependable method, given that they may at best play a couple of rounds a week, belong to a club with rudimentary or non-existent practice facilities, and may very well be using implements which, in their case, are indeed ill-suited to their humble purpose. The point is that golf, of all the still-ball games, is the most difficult because of the multiplicity of factors beyond the players' control.

Put-upon is a charitable description of the lot of club golfers. They cannot influence the bounce which diverts the ball into a hazard instead of avoiding it; they cannot escape the unfairness of an awkward fairway lie while an opponent, only feet away and perhaps in the rough, has no such problem. A degree of stoicism, of acceptance of fate's fickle finger, is essential for survival. Did not Greg Norman, otherwise an example to us all, once allege that he smothered a drive when, committed to his downswing, a worm popped up behind the ball?

All golfers have their fantasies and this one's has for some time now, as what powers he ever had continue their irreversible decline, been this. How much better would he score if a tournament professional of Norman's reputation for being both the longest and straightest driver in the game, hit all his tee-shots for him? The sneaking feeling persists that the improvement would not be as exceptional as might be imagined or hoped for. The reason for that gloomy view rests in the word fear — fear of the consequences of making a better than usual start or of a good score in the making being unravelled by a faltering step towards the end.

These two perceptions were brought together years ago by Henry Longhurst when he declared that the only games in which average golfers were remotely concerned were (a) those of the leading tournament professionals of the time and (b) their own. In between these lay a no-man's land grazed over not so much by hostility as by indifference. And so it is that this anthology seeks to draw together a wide range of topics calculated to interest and help this game's backbone, golfers at large. Whether or not they benefit is up to them; ultimately all golfers must make their own salvations. Every golfer, no matter what his place in the game's pecking order, is ultimately alone in the crowd.

TAKE A TIP

Club golfers are invariably on the lookout for the miracle cure that will transform their game even though, deep down, they know there is no such thing. However, tinkering with a swing is all part of the attraction of the game and our tips, from 33 different professionals, are given in this spirit. Advice generally is to try a new idea first on the practice area rather than the course and to see whether it works for you. This is particularly the case with putting, which can be highly individual. It is worth noting that the technique of professionals in this book differs.

It cannot be emphasised strongly enough that if you have a golfing ailment, there is no substitute for taking a lesson, or series of lessons from your club professional. He is the one with the experience and knowledge to diagnose and correct the fault.

Our tips have been put in various groups — address, grip and posture; drills and exercises; long game; keep straight; bunker play; short game; and problem shots. It should also be underlined that this is by no means a course of instruction, simply a compilation of individual tips requested and willingly provided by courtesy of the professionals concerned.

We start with the swing many of us wish we had and arguably the most admired in the world, that of Spanish maestro Severiano Ballesteros, and an appreciation of it by prominent Scottish amateur Charlie Green. That is the model. Aim for it by all means, but don't be disappointed if you never manage to come even remotely close to it . . . The photographs were taken at Westerwood near Cumbernauld, the course Ballesteros has co-designed. He is using a No. 7 iron for a shot of 147 yards.

Severiano Ballesteros has a swing close to perfection which is what you

13

A relaxed start to the downswing

Wrists still cocked

Powering into the ball

would expect from a player of the calibre of an Open champion. The one thing that surprises me is the shape of his left arm which, on the downswing is far from straight.

Look at the way it is bent in the first and second pictures. It is certainly a lesson to amateurs that a straight left arm does not mean a rigid one as is commonly thought. I am sure this is something that is natural with him. He will probably feel it is straight and it is only the relaxed nature of his swing, a point highlighted in John McTear's tip, which causes this position. The club selection also indicates that he is hitting well within himself.

The point can be taken further. The most important section of the swing is from 18 inches before impact to the completed follow through. Many amateurs make far too much effort on the backswing.

The tendency of most amateurs is to take a wide backswing, but that probably makes the throughswing too shallow. What can be taken out of these photographs is that amateurs should be thinking of a wider

Start of the extension *A balanced, high finish* *A different angle on the extended follow through*

swing *through* the ball. The purpose of a backswing is merely to put the club in a position where a good downswing can be made. There is no great effort needed to do this.

The third picture shows his left arm much straighter, and look at the extension of the swing on the follow through. Most amateurs manage an extension as far as the position in the fourth picture but lose it thereafter. Picture six, taken from a different angle, shows that Seve has managed to maintain that extension to a point where the follow through is above his shoulders.

The question may be asked what does it matter what happens after impact — the ball is away by then? The answer is that the shape of the follow through is determined by what has happened at impact. Stretching towards the target area will give much greater control.

Other points to look at are the position of the wrists in relation to the club in the first and second pictures. They are identical. In the second, halfway through the downswing, the wrists are still fully cocked. The power is all there waiting to be unleashed through impact, as is happening in the third picture.

Also look at the way Seve drives his legs through the ball. Nothing much has happened in the first picture, the weight is still quite evenly distributed. The transfer of weight to the left foot is starting on the second and continues right through to the completed follow through at which point he has cleared his side out and round into a balanced finish with the hands nice and high.

It is interesting to note how his left heel never comes off the ground, a technique which gives good control if you are supple. If not, you must let the heel rise.

Without doubt it is the swing of a champion.

The addresses and telephone numbers of those whose tips appear are:

Brian Anderson, Dalmahoy Golf Hotel & Country Club, Kirknewton, Midlothian. 031 333 1436.
Andy Armstrong, Fereneze Golf Club, Barrhead, Renfrewshire. 041 880 7058.
Anthony Caira, Kirriemuir Golf Club, Kirriemuir, Angus. 0575 73317.
Niall Cameron, Royal St George's Golf Club, Sandwich, Kent. 0304 617380.
Bob Collinson, Windyhill Golf Club, Windyhill, Bearsden, Dunbartonshire. 041 942 7157.
Frank Coutts, Deeside Golf Club, Bieldside, Aberdeen. 0224 861041.
Robert Craig, Cardross Golf Club, Cardross, Dunbartonshire. 0389 841350.
John Easey, Ayr Belleisle Golf Club, Ayr. 0292 41314.
Campbell Elliott, Clydebank & District Golf Club, Hardgate, Clydebank. 041 952 8769.
Maureen Garner, Hill Valley Golf Hotel & Country Club, Terrick Road, Whitchurch, Shropshire. 0948 3032.
Ronnie Gregan, Crow Wood Golf Club, Muirhead, Chryston, Glasgow. 041 779 1943.
Cliffe Jones, Glencorse Golf Club, Milton Bridge, Penicuik, Midlothian. 0968 76481.
Kenneth Kelly, Baberton Golf Club, Juniper Green, Edinburgh. 031 453 3361.
Alex Marshall, 22 Farragon Drive, Aberfeldy, Tayside. 0887 20910.
John Mulgrew, Normandy Driving Range, Inchinnan Road, Renfrew. 041 886 7477.
Jim McAlister, Haggs Castle Golf Club, 70 Dumbreck Road, Glasgow. 041 427 3355.

Ronnie MacAskill, Royal Aberdeen Golf Club, Balgownie, Bridge of Don, Aberdeen. 0224 702221.

Jim McCallum, Lenzie Golf Club, 19 Crosshill Road, Lenzie, Dunbartonshire. 041 777 7748.

George McKay, Glenbervie Golf Club, Stirling Road, Larbert, Stirlingshire. 0324 562725.

Brian MacKenzie, Bruntsfield Links Golfing Society, 32 Barnton Avenue, Edinburgh. 031 336 4050.

Alastair McLean, Duddingston Golf Club, Duddingston, Edinburgh. 031 661 4301.

John McTear, Cowgler Golf Club, 301 Barrhead Road, Glasgow. 041 649 9401.

Iain Parker, Prestwick St Nicholas Golf Club, Grangemuir Road, Prestwick, Ayrshire. 0292 79755.

Ian Rae, Hollandbush Golf Club, Acre Tophead, Lesmahagow, by Coalburn. 0555 983646.

Graham Ross, Greenock Golf Club, Forsyth Street, Greenock. 0475 87236.

Douglas Smart, Banchory Golf Club, Kinneskie, Banchory, Kincardineshire. 03302 2447.

Kevin Stables, Professional, Ranfurly Castle Golf Club, Golf Road, Bridge of Weir. 0505 614795.

Gillian Stewart, Claremont Business Equipment, 112 Cornwall Street South, Glasgow. 041 427 5364.

Peter Thomson, Erskine Golf Club, Bishopton, Renfrewshire. 0505 862108.

Ron Wallace, Lanark Golf Club, The Moor, Lanark. 0555 61456.

Alistair Webster, Montrose Golf Club, Traill Drive, Montrose. 0674 72634.

Gary Weir, Elderslie Golf Club, Elderslie, Renfrewshire. 0505 20032.

Kevan Whitson, Turnhouse Golf Club, 154 Turnhouse Road, Edinburgh. 031 339 7701.

ADDRESS, GRIP AND POSTURE

KENNETH KELLY

Tilt From Your Waist for a Good Posture

Poor posture at address is one of the most common faults that I come across in the handicap golfer. The knees being too bent, a straight, vertical back, and a chin tucked into the body are an all too common sight.

In order to maintain the height that will produce, automatically, a wider arc and more powerful swing, the chin should be kept well away from the chest and the knees should be flexed but comfortable. And, most important of all, the player should tilt forward from the waist. Try to imagine that the buckle of your belt is pointing towards the ball.

From the correct position it is much easier to initiate a proper turning action, transferring the weight on to the right side, and the desired rotational movement that produces a 90 degree turn of the shoulders.

A poor posture tends to lead to the club lifting at the start of the backswing. Remember, the club should be kept low and swept back from the ball.

The purpose of the backswing is to set the player in position for a powerful attack on the ball, and everything stems from having a good posture.

A good idea is to practise the set-up position, side on, in front of a mirror. Keep the knees flexed, tilt forward from the waist — you should almost feel as though your bottom is sticking out! — and keep the chin up.

● Kenneth Kelly, the professional at Baberton, is stockist of all leading golf equipment and clothing. Tuition by appointment.

Kenneth Kelly demonstrates a poor posture. The chin is tucked into the body, the back is vertical, and the knees are too bent

This picture shows a good posture, chin out, knees comfortably flexed, and belt buckle pointing towards the ball

ALISTAIR McLEAN

Keeping on the Ball at Address

A common fault among handicap golfers who come to me for lessons is a wrong position of the ball at address in relation to their feet. Their tendency is to have the ball too far forward.

This means the hands are likely to be behind the ball at impact. The effect of this will be a slice or pulled shot. Most high handicappers do not manage to keep their head still because, with the ball in a forward position, they have to move forward to make contact thereby producing a damaging out-to-in swingpath.

Occasionally a golfer will have the ball too far back in the stance in which case the reverse will be the case. The hands will get ahead of the ball, the swing will be in-to-out, and the result is likely to be a push or hooked shot.

As a general rule the ball should be one third of the way back from the left foot in the stance for No. 5 to No. 9 iron shots. With the advent of No. 5 and No. 7 woods, club golfers are making less use of irons from No. 4 down but if the longer irons are used the ball should be slightly further forward.

For wooden clubs the ball should be opposite the left heel so that impact is achieved at the start of the upswing. For wedge or sand wedge shots it is vital to have the hands ahead of the ball at impact, therefore the ball should be nearer the right foot at address.

It is worthwhile having these ball positions checked regularly because it is hard to see the position yourself. It does not need to be your professional who does this. Your playing partner will be able to tell you exactly where the ball is to enable you to make any necessary adjustment.

● Alastair McLean is the professional at Duddingston.

RIGHT . . . Alastair McLean has the ball inside his left foot at address for an iron shot and returns to the same position at impact without swaying

WRONG . . . the ball is too far forward in the stance and a sway forward is required to make contact with the probable result of a slice or pulled shot

JOHN EASEY

Beware of Your Grip Slipping to the Right

When golfers, whether they are experienced or have only recently learned the game, come to me and say they are not hitting the ball straight. I always tell them they must look at the basics. That is, grip, stance and address position, most importantly the grip.

For the correct grip the left thumb should be down the centre of the clubshaft and the back of the left hand facing the target. The right hand should be over the left hand with the back facing away from the target. As long as the grip remains firm the clubface should return to the same position at impact.

A common fault is for the grip to slip to the right. That will cause the clubface to close on impact causing the ball to fly left, sometimes off the heel, and very low.

To achieve the correct stance and address position, your weight should be evenly distributed and your feet should be apart by approximately the width of the shoulders. Feet, hips and shoulders should all be parallel to the line of target.

These principles are true even at the very highest level of the game. On the evening before Greg Norman, the leader, went into the final round of the Open Championship at Turnberry, Jack Nicklaus offered him some advice. It was nothing fanciful about attitude of mind. He said simply: 'Check the pressure on your grip before every shot.' Basics again.

Norman went out the next day and won. This tip might not elevate you to that level, but it might prevent a few disasters in your next medal round!

● John Easey is the professional at Ayr Belleisle.

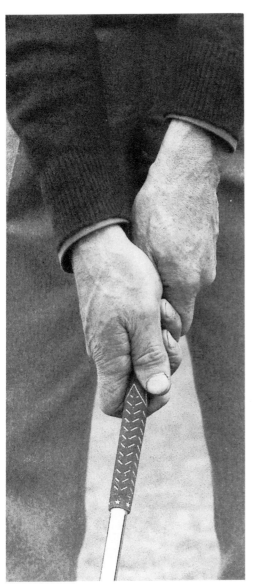

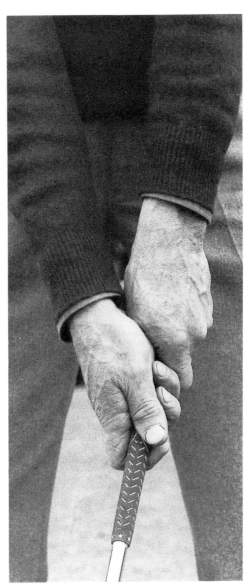

RIGHT . . . John Easey's grip at address, with the back of the left hand facing the target

WRONG . . . note how the left hand has slipped towards the right. This grip is likely to take you off the straight and narrow

ALISTAIR WEBSTER

Firm Up Your Grip

One of the most common faults among handicap players is that when hitting full shots the hands tend to separate on the backswing.

If the right hand opens on the backswing (top) it will inevitably lead to an early and over-exaggerated cock of the wrists. The fault usually produces a poor, weak, flicking action that causes the ball to 'leak' out to the right or can produce an equally damaging 'thin' shot. These are just two examples, but letting go with the right hand can result in a multitude of bad shots.

To overcome the problem the right hand should act as a valley, encasing the thumb of the left hand. Increase the pressure on top of the left thumb at address and maintain that throughout the swing. Do not grip too tightly, but make sure that the hands never come away from the club.

If you do succeeed in maintaining a firmer contact it will improve your striking, especially with the long and middle irons.

● **Alistair Webster is the professional at Montrose.**

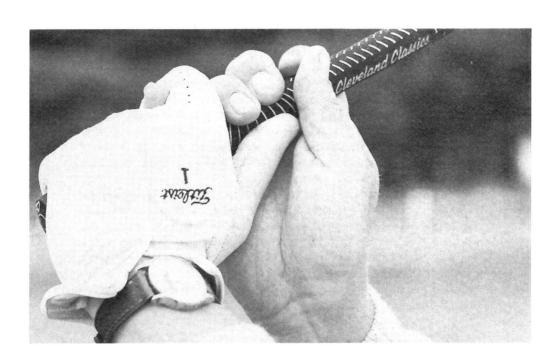

JOHN McTEAR

Loosen Up and Use a Constant Grip Pressure

A common fault I have found among golfers in the higher handicap range is tensing up on shots. The shoulders hunch up, the arms become rigid, and the grip tightens. With such a posture there is no chance of generating sufficient clubhead speed to execute a decent shot.

I call them the white-knuckle brigade and they also come to grief on the short pitch shot for which their arms are so tense that the club stops very quickly after impact. There is no follow through to speak of and the ball could go anywhere.

The answer is simply to loosen those muscles. The best example I know of a perfectly relaxed, yet controlled, address is Severiano Ballesteros. Make a point of watching him the next time you see him on television. By copying him your results are unlikely to be as good as his, but you will be giving yourself every chance of a big improvement.

An experiment carried out recently in America illustrates the problem scientifically. Electrodes, which can detect the slightest tensing or easing of muscles, were attached to the arms of a 15-handicapper and a professional. The graph of the handicapper's swing was highly irregular whereas the professional's graph was flat.

The problem exists to a lesser extent among low handicap golfers to whom my advice is to try and achieve a constant grip pressure for every shot.

● John McTear, the professional at Cowglen, reminds readers that you don't need to be a member of a golf club to take advantage of the services provided by a PGA professional.

RIGHT . . . this relaxed posture is much more likely to produce a good shot

WRONG . . . John McTear exaggerates the damaging hunched-shoulder method

JIM McALISTER

Keep Your Head Behind the Ball

Head position is vital for the correct execution of a golf shot and the best time to study the technique of the world's top players is the Open Championship, especially in the television slow-motion replays.

Watch how the head is kept behind the ball, in the same position, from address through to impact. The only one of the top players who does not adhere to this rule is Curtis Strange, who moves his head to the right on the backswing, but at impact it has returned to where it was at address.

That method works for Strange, but you would not be well advised to do the same. Concentrate on keeping your head behind the ball all the time. A common fault of handicap golfers is a lateral sway in which the head and shoulders move to the left on the downswing. The club follows an out-to-in path with the likely result of a slice or pulled shot. It also cuts down on distance as much of the body has moved ahead of the ball before impact.

It is important to make a full shoulder turn, keeping the club on the inside on the downswing. A stationary head will help you get through the ball and is more likely to keep you on the fairway. If you see Open golfers in trouble you might be able to spot the fault yourself.

● **John Letters, staff player, Jim McAlister is the professional at Haggs Castle.**

*STEADY HEAD . . . Jim McAlister shows the head position as it should be
both at address and impact — behind the ball*

BOB COLLINSON

Good Takeaway Will Put You in the Swing

For many years I have been teaching what I call the one-piece takeaway. It is not a tip in any gimmicky sense. I believe it is an absolute fundamental.

First of all, imagine a right-angled cross at your feet, or even place two clubs on the ground in this position. The line pointing away from the inside of your left heel is the guide to your straight left arm and the club itself, which should be a continuation of that line. The other line is pointing towards the target.

Now stand tall and do not stretch. Posture is of great importance. You will be looking down at the ball but your head will not be pointing down. Keep your head steady but not solid. This is the position you want to be in when the clubhead returns to the ball. It is your starting point and no matter what you do thereafter, there is no reason why you cannot at least set yourself up as well as Tom Weiskopf or Seve Ballesteros.

If you do not, you are putting yourself at a big disadvantage. It is the position which dictates what is going to happen.

Then try the one-piece takeaway. That means taking the club back naturally, turning with both shoulders which will take you on an inside line, opening the clubface. Do not *try* to take an inside line, it will happen itself. And the one-piece, or one-movement takeaway will make the shoulders and hips turn and set up a full swing arc. Thereafter, try to cultivate a good tempo, finishing the swing with your belt buckle pointing to the target and weight completely transferred to the left.

● Bob Collinson, the professional at Windyhill, is available for expert tuition by appointment plus video lessons.

At address (top left) the line pointing away is the guide to your straight left arm and the club which is a continuation of it. Then take the club back naturally on an inside line, turning both shoulders (top right). At the completion of the downswing (right) finish with your front towards the target

DRILLS AND EXERCISES

FRANK COUTTS

A Firm Wrist for a Better Short Game

In playing short shots, both pitching and putting, the most common fault is the collapse of the left wrist at impact. This can cause a number of poor shots, including the thinned and sclaffed variety.

On playing pitch shots the stance and hips should be slightly open, with the shoulders kept square to the target line. The player should feel comfortable — stay relaxed.

The weight should be 75 per cent on the left leg, 25 per cent on the right, and that distribution should be maintained throughout the swing.

Your are now in position to play the pitch. Swing through the ball, ensuring that the left wrist is kept firm throughout the shot.

The collapse of the left wrist in the putting stroke is equally damaging. Swing the arms, do not hinge the wrists.

When practising pitch shots, a good trick is to place a comb behind your watch. This will act as a splint over the wrist. It will now be impossible for the left wrist to break during the shot.

Similarly, when practising putting, use the right hand, by grasping the left forearm, to clamp the left arm and hand to the putter. Once again, it will be impossible for the left wrist to collapse during the stroke.

● North-East regional coach, Frank Coutts is the professional at Deeside, sponsored by Vauxhall Opel dealer Lawrence of Kemnay and stockist of Macgregor, Mizuno, Dunlop, Taylor-Made, La Coste and Sergio Tacchini goods.

(Top left) In pitching practice, a comb behind your watch will prevent collapse of the left wrist

(Top right) Stance and hips should be open with 75 per cent of your weight on the left leg

(Right) In putting, grasping the left forearm will clamp the left arm and hand to the club

ANTHONY CAIRA

Be a Weight Watcher

Proper weight transference is one of the most vital components of a good, well-balanced golf swing.

The weight should move on to the right foot during the backswing and transfer to the left foot on the follow through. The correct movement of weight will produce a well-balanced position at the conclusion of the swing.

All too often, the club golfer makes the mistake of keeping all the weight on the left side on the backswing, which is reflected in an off-balance position through impact and the follow through. Having completed the swing, the player will fall back on to the right side. The result of this bad action is a severe slice or a shot hit off the heel.

To overcome the problem I would suggest the following drill:

Using a No. 6 iron, tee the ball up opposite the left heel. Swing to waist height on the backswing — stop and 'feel' the weight on the right foot.

Now swing through to waist height on the follow through, 'kicking' the right knee towards the target at impact. The weight at the completion of the follow through should be entirely on the left foot.

Keep practising the drill until the action becomes automatic.

● Anthony Caira, the professional at Kirriemuir, is stockist of Pringle, Wilson, Mizuno and other big name goods. Tuition, including use of special video equipment, is available at all times.

WEIGHT on the right foot at backswing   *TRANSFERRING to left at follow through*

BRIAN MacKENZIE

Full Turn of the Shoulders is Vital

The basic fault of club golfers is a failure to make a full turn of the shoulders on the backswing. If you don't get it right going back, it will never be right coming down.

A full wind-up enables the player to get the body through before the clubhead and, therefore, have the hips and legs working properly. A poor shoulder turn usually results in the player hitting from the top, coming across the ball and the outcome is a damaging cut shot.

The following faults are inevitable when the player fails to make a full shoulder turn on the backswing — the left shoulder stays ahead of the ball, the hands are too high and the back faces left of target.

With the correct action, at the top of the backswing, the left shoulder should be behind the ball and the back and clubhead should be pointing towards the target.

There is a tip that I recommend to help create the correct action. As shown in the picture, place the club between the arms across the back. Keeping the head in place, swing round until the left shoulder is under the chin and the clubhead is pointing at the ball. Groove this action through practice, and then try to repeat it on the course.

● **Brian MacKenzie is the professional at Bruntsfield Links Golf Club.**

JOHN MULGREW

Steady up for a Better Swing

A driving range where you have a constantly flat surface is ideal for developing a repetitive swing. Yet all that many people do is use a driver, full out, to hit their entire bucket of balls. There is a certain enjoyment in this, but there are better ways of using the range to improve your game.

Many handicap golfers have a body sway, especially on the back-swing. A tip to cure this is to hit a series of balls with your feet together. With your feet apart you may realise your fault but be unable to do anything about it. Feet together, a sway will knock you completely off-balance and you will be forced into the right kind of pivot if you are to hit the ball at all.

Golf is a game of feel. Many golfers make the mistake of hitting at the ball instead of through it. A bonus in having your feet together is that it helps the pace of the swing, will release tension, and help develop rhythm and tempo.

Try it with a variety of clubs, not just your driver. And at a driving range, of course, there is the benefit of not having to collect the balls afterwards.

● John Mulgrew, the professional at Normandy Driving Range, is stockist of an extensive range of golf equipment by all leading manufacturers.

FAULT . . . John Mulgrew spots a symptom of the sway, the protruding left knee of Dr Iain Blackwood, a 9-handicapper at Glasgow

CURE . . . feet together, the doc-turned-patient is forced to make a correctly balanced follow through

IAN RAE

Central Control Key to Swing Arc

The trunk should play the dominant role in the swing. Many handicap players make the mistake of using the hands to control the body and that way there is likely to be a lot of unnecessary movement, with the result that the ball could go just about anywhere.

A simple exercise is to grip the club normally, then press the end of the shaft against the stomach with the clubhead pointing straight out (top left). Then turn 45 degrees, so that shoulders and stomach are still pointing in the same direction. The clubhead should still be pointing directly away from you (top right). If the hands have been used the end of the club will have come away from the stomach (right).

Now try it with a proper swing. Stop yourself partly up the backswing and check if the club is pointing away in a straight line from your stomach. If it is not, your hands have come into action too soon. As with all swing changes, try it out on the practice area before doing it on the course.

A way of picturing what is happening is to imagine the clubhead as the outside of a wheel, and you the inside. It is the centre that is in control, and the quicker you turn in the middle, the greater will be the speed on the outside.

The greatest example of this technique is Nick Faldo. A few years ago he had a lot of hand movement, now he has virtually none, and look at the tremendous shape his game is in. But it took a long time before this adjustment worked for him, so do not despair if you do not find an immediate improvement.

● Ian Rae is the professional at Hollandbush.

LONG GAME

GEORGE YUILLE

A Shorter Swing to go a Long Way

Many handicap golfers have a tendency to try for the 'big one', especially off the tee. What they normally do to try and achieve this is over-swing in the mistaken belief that this will give them more distance. This way a destructive shot is much more likely with the ball ending up in deep trouble.

The club does not have to go beyond being parallel to the ground for extra length. Concentrate more on achieving a 90 degree shoulder turn and swing the club rather than allow the club to swing you.

The key to a successful backswing is control, knowing how far you can take the club back and never going beyond that point. The effect will be a more controlled golf shot and hopefully this will be combined with the extra distance you are looking for.

● George Yuille is the professional at the Royal Burgess Golfing Society.

RIGHT . . . out of sight could be the result of this swing. George Yuille is in perfect control after a 90 degree shoulder turn. The club is not beyond being parallel with the ground

WRONG . . . out of bounds is the likely outcome with this effort. The over-swing might make you feel strong but the posture is unwieldy and there is little control

ALEX MARSHALL

Secret of the Long Downhill Shot

Many Scottish courses are hilly in character and, inevitably, the player will be faced with an uphill or downhill lie. Even on the beautiful Taymouth Castle course which is mainly flat, the player is, more often than not, faced with a long downhill second on the 12th and a shortish uphill second on the 13th. It is the former which poses the greater problem.

The classic 'weight on the uphill foot' cliché does not work too well where the player has to strike flat out with something like a No. 3 wood to achieve the required distance. The ball is very often topped.

Rather, the emphasis should be placed on aligning the shoulder-line parallel with the slope and playing the ball from the middle of the stance. This will allow the clubhead to follow the contour of the ground right through the ball and, at the same time, minimise the left-to-right movement of the ball inherent in the stroke.

Try it next time you are in this position.

● **Alex Marshall has retired as professional at Taymouth Castle but is still available for lessons.**

RIGHT . . . Alex Marshall's shoulders parallel with the slope, and weight evenly distributed

WRONG . . . the weight is on the uphill foot and the likely result will be a topped shot

GRAHAM ROSS

Point with your Left Knee

Your left knee is a key to hitting the ball longer and straighter off the tee. The secret is to ensure that the knee is pointing in towards the ball on the backswing thereby providing a basis for a fuller, more controlled and powerful swing. Failure to do so will restrict the swing, putting the club in a laid-off position after the top of the backswing, i.e. the shaft pointing to the left. This will cause an outside-to-inside, across-the-line downswing with the most likely result being a pull or a slice.

There are other matters to consider and I recommend following three points.

1. At address, body alignment should be slightly left of target so as to allow you a little more room to get through the shot later in the swing. Grip pressure should be slight as this will relax the muscles in your forearms and allow you to release the clubhead through the ball with greater speed.

2. Make sure you have a one-piece takeaway back from the ball by taking the left arm and shaft back in one unit for the first three feet of the backswing before the gradual cocking of the wrists. This movement along with the left knee pointing in towards the back of the ball will give you the basis for a bigger turn and swing arc.

3. The previous movements of the takeaway will have put the weight slightly on your right foot at the top of the backswing. With the downswing and release of the hands and arms through the hitting area, the weight should be driven through to your left side. This movement will have given you a bigger arc through the ball, allowing you to get all your bodyweight behind the shot.

● Graham Ross, the professional at Greenock, is sponsored by Kilmaurs Engineering.

READY FOR THE BIG HIT . . . Graham Ross demonstrates how an inward-pointing left knee allows a fuller, more controlled swing

NIALL CAMERON
Swing Shorter for Better Control in Winter

As winter approaches and the air temperature drops, you are going to find yourself struggling to hit the ball as far as you did in summer. Many amateurs make the mistake of trying to make up for this by hitting the ball harder, often with disastrous results. What is needed is a little self-discipline. Accept that you are not going to hit the ball so far and instead try to swing the club better.

Remember, too, that in winter we all wear more clothing and frequently, in addition, a waterproof suit. These restrict the swing so compensation must be made. Shortening your swing will allow you greater control. If in good weather you have a full backswing, try a three-quarter swing. If you already have a short swing, try shortening it further.

This is especially important if you are playing a shot into a strong, cold wind under which circumstances you will need to keep the ball low. Try gripping the club further down the shaft. The combination of the low grip and shorter swing will help keep the ball down, and if you want to hit lower still, take up an address position with the ball nearer the right foot which will have the effect of decreasing the loft of the club. A few other preparations will help to keep your score down.

1. Ask your club professional to recommend the correct ball. I would suggest using a wound ball in preference to a solid ball. As the temperature drops, golf balls become more difficult to compress and therefore you should also switch to a lower compression ball.

2. Change golf balls on alternate holes, keeping the spare ball warm in your pocket. Remember to inform your partner though when you change on the tee.

3. If you wear a glove, try taking it off between shots. The glove is designed to give you a better grip on the club, so if you pick up a wet bag or tend the pin in the rain while wearing it, you will immediately have a slippery contact and there will be a greater risk of losing control.

4. Check you have a towel in your bag to dry your grips between shots.

5. You may also wish at this time of year to invest in new grips from which you would constantly benefit. Your only link with the club is through the grip and it is much easier to hold on to a soft, tacky grip than an old, worn slippery one. Again, ask your club professional to fit the correct size of grip for your own hand size. Too thin a grip is as bad as a worn one.

DRY WEATHER SWING . . . unrestricted, Niall Cameron takes a full backswing and goes for distance. Gripping at the end of the club will help you to hit the ball harder

WET WEATHER SWING . . . waterproofs on, a three-quarter swing will help keep you straight. Grip down the shaft and address the ball back in the stance to stay low

● Niall Cameron, the professional at Royal St George's, plays and recommends Slazenger golf equipment, including the new Seve Ballesteros forged irons.

ANDY ARMSTRONG

Relaxed Swing the Key to Distance

The majority of club golfers watch the game on television and one aspect of the professional swing which I recommend trying to emulate is the uninhibited release of the clubhead.

Almost all higher handicap players are amazed at the relative ease with which top professionals swing the club and the vast distances they send the ball. Are they twice as strong as club golfers? Of course not.

The average golfer stands on the tee with muscles bulging, forearms tight as a drum, ready to launch the ball a huge distance. The backswing is short and quick, and the downswing and follow through are shorter and quicker still.

This is in stark contrast to the majority of top professionals who, addressing the ball in a relaxed and comfortable position, take the club back from the ball in an unhurried manner to complete a full backswing. The downswing is just as unhurried. Rather than the lunge so typical of many amateurs, the professionals allow their hands and arms to swing smoothly on the downswing and let the clubhead release freely through impact, carrying them on to a long, well-balanced follow through.

It is this uninhibited release of the clubhead which enables professionals to hit the ball so far, and it is worth a close look.

The clubhead will only release freely through the ball if allowed to do so. If the grip is tight and the forearms tense, the clubhead will be restricted from releasing freely through the ball. This results in a short follow through and a poor shot to match.

Club golfers should, therefore, try and swing the club in a more relaxed and rhythmical manner, making sure you have a long, well-balanced follow through. This should result in a longer, straighter shot with less effort.

● **Andy Armstrong is the professional at Fereneze.**

Andy Armstrong demonstrates (top right) the uninhibited clubhead release which has carried his hands and arms through and towards a long, balanced follow through and (right) the common fault of handicap golfers — tight grip, tense forearms and a restricted release. Compare both with the downswing position (top left). The proper release will have turned the hands and clubface through 180 degrees, the faulty one will have turned barely 90 degrees

KEEP STRAIGHT

IAIN PARKER
Keep Your Right Arm Low to Hit Straight
More than 80 per cent of good golf stems from the pre-shot routine and the first two feet of the backswing. Most golfers think that if their feet are pointing towards the target that is all they have to do in the way of alignment. They never think of their shoulders.

Equally, if not more important than the feet, is correct alignment of the shoulders. That is what controls the line of the swing. The natural tendency is for the right shoulder to protrude. That way, however, the initial movement of the club is outside the correct line resulting in an out-to-in swing across the target line. The probable result will be a slice or a pulled shot.

A useful tip which I have found helps many handicap golfers is to ensure that the right elbow and forearm are lower than the left when viewed from behind. To achieve this I put a club between the arms with the shaft positioned in front of the right arm and behind the left. That helps the pupil into position and when I remove the club the shoulders should be square which will help start the clubhead back on the correct line.

● Iain Parker is the professional at Prestwich St Nicholas, and a leading stockist in Ayrshire of Mizuno, Taylor-Made, Ram and Ben Sayers equipment.

ON THE RIGHT LINES . . . Iain Parker puts John Leishman, the 10-handicap club secretary, on the straight and narrow by using a golf club to force his right forearm below his left

GEORGE McKAY

Turn, Don't Tilt

Probably the most common fault among handicap golfers is the slice. One of the major causes of this is tilting instead of turning the shoulders on the backswing.

Many players tend to dip at the start of the backswing causing the club to go back too steeply and outside the intended line with the result of an extreme out-to-in downswing.

The cure is to make sure your left shoulder is turned behind the ball whilst maintaining height and posture. The result will be a more rounded swing allowing a proper transfer of weight and producing the desired in-to-out swingpath.

● **George McKay is the professional at Glenbervie.**

RIGHT . . . George McKay's left shoulder has turned so that it is behind the ball

WRONG . . . the shoulders are tilted, the posture is unwieldly. A slice is the likely result

RONNIE GREGAN

Inside Line will Lead to Correct Club Path

Many players are under the misconception that the path of the golf swing follows a straight line back and through. But nothing could be further from the truth.

In order to carry out the correct leg, hip, and shoulder turn — which generates the power in the swing, the clubhead must travel inside on the backswing, back to square at impact, and then inside again on the follow through.

Two of the most common faults are caused by not turning properly.

1. **Reverse pivot.** If the player tries to keep the club on a straight line going back then the shoulders will tilt instead of turn, throwing all the weight on to the left foot. The process is reversed on the downswing and the player inevitably loses balance and falls backwards on to the right side. The resultant shot lacks power and is often struck 'thin'.

2. **Coming over the top.** This occurs when the legs lock and the top half of the body takes over, casting the club on an outward plane. The damaging outcome is a snap hook.

In order to strike the ball well, the player must achieve proper weight transference and that can only be gained by co-ordinating the leg, hip, and shoulder turn. It is no use just swiping at the ball with the arms and hands.

● Ronnie Gregan is the professional at Crow Wood, where lessons and all golf requisites are available.

Ronnie Gregan demonstrates the resultant loss of balance at impact from taking a straight line on the backswing

An inside line will lead to a proper, balanced transfer of weight

DOUGLAS SMART

Hinge Holds Key to Success

I try to emphasise that there are three swings, which encompass the 'Swing Hinge'. They are the normal swing, sand swing, and wood swing. The hand action for all shots is not the same, otherwise hitting a driver would be as easy as hitting a No. 7 iron. I find the most common occurrence is slicing with the driver, while pulling the No. 7 iron. This is due to the difference in design from woods to irons, and to compensate for this in-built effect, a golfer's hand action should be on the following lines:

1. **Normal Swing** (top left) — Use the normal backswing, and a full release of hands. The clubface will be square at impact, and the hands in line with the ball. This gives good clubhead speed and a normal trajectory.

2. **Sand Swing** (top right) — Again the normal backswing. The hands are kept in front of the shaft at, and after, impact. There should be no release, i.e. the clubhead does not pass the hands. A steep angle of attack with the clubface open giving little clubhead speed will produce a high trajectory.

3. **Wood Swing** (right) — This seems to cause most problems with the average amateur. It's important that the left wrist hinges during this shot, rather than the normal roll of the wrists, which will produce a low, left shot. The hands will be behind the clubhead at impact, and the clubface must be square. This will provide a shallow angle of attack and a lower trajectory. To simulate the correct position with a driver, stand with the hands well behind the ball and the clubface pointing to the target. You will feel the hinge at the back of your left hand, and there will appear to be extra loft on the clubface.

Note: Any of these swings can be used with any club. Examples: Use the 'sand swing' with a No. 3 iron and a low, cutting shot will result — a useful shot from a bad lie, perhaps. Use the 'wood swing' with a sand wedge and you will either get a Lee Trevino bladed shot, or the more desirable, extremely high shot.

● **Douglas Smart is the professional at Banchory Golf Club.**

KEVIN STABLES

Hit Past Your Chin to Avoid Shanking

The shank is one of the most destructive and soul-destroying shots in golf. The cause and cure were best explained to me by Tony Jacklin at a clinic I attended while still a young assistant at Turnberry and it is his method that I have used with success in my teaching career.

A player shanks when the head and top half of the body move ahead of the ball. This is caused in the main by standing too close to or too far away from the ball, or by trying to force the ball into the air. The hands and clubface become too open and the shot careers off at about a 45 degree angle to the right.

The remedy is to make sure that the club and right shoulder hit past the chin. In other words, let the clubhead do the work.

Shanking is also a mental problem. Having hit one such shot the natural reaction is — panic! The over-anxious player looks up to see where the next shot is going, which, with the top half of the body swaying forward, is inevitably in the same direction.

Alternatively, the victim tries to compensate by rolling the wrists over, but only succeeds in pulling the shot to the left.

A helpful hint is to imagine there is a spike travelling straight down through your head and spine to the ground. Keep the spine still and let the rest of the body turn around it. Remember, the loft of the clubface will lift the ball in the air — let the club do the work.

● **Kevin Stables is the professional at Ranfurly Castle.**

Shanking is caused by the head and body moving ahead of the ball

The ball has been left in the photo to show that the head should remain directly above the point of impact

BUNKER PLAY

BRIAN ANDERSON

Playing out of a Bunker

Many handicap golfers have a fear of playing out of bunkers. This fear can adversely affect not only the shot from the sand. If a player is afraid of going into a bunker it will also mean that the approach shot to a green heavily guarded by bunkers will be played with less confidence. Once a golfer is proficient at recovering from sand, the approach shot will become less off-putting. For these reasons every player should take time to practise greenside bunker shots.

Every golfer should have in his bag a sand iron — a splash club purely for bunker play. I frequently see golfers trying to get out of bunkers with a No. 9 iron or a pitching wedge, which makes the shot even more difficult.

(Left) I have given myself a good stance by wriggling my feet in the sand. Doing so also gives the player a good indication of the sand's texture. The ball is positioned opposite the left heel, my stance is slightly open to create a natural out-to-in swingpath, and my hands are well down the shaft to allow a steeper-than-usual backswing to achieve the necessary elevation on the ball. The sand is dry so I am aiming about two inches behind the ball. If the sand is wet, reduce that distance to one inch.

(Middle) The splash shows that I have connected with the sand and not the ball. It is important that the head remains absolutely still. Any movement is likely to result in taking too much sand and the ball will finish well short of the flag. The swing should be smooth and rhythmical.

(Right) One of the most important aspects of the bunker shot is the follow through. A common fault among handicap golfers is that they stop immediately after impact. The club should be swung well through the ball to a high finish which is more likely to produce the desired result.

There are two ways of controlling the length of the shot. The player can either retain the same length of backswing for every shot and take less sand for a longer shot, more for shorter, or he can take the same amount of sand every time and take a longer swing for more distance, shorter for less.

● **Brian Anderson, the professional at Dalmahoy Golf Hotel and Country Club, is one of Scotland's most experienced tutors. The new development at Dalmahoy is a country club hotel establishment, with more than 100 bedrooms, offering golf and leisure facilities of the highest quality.**

GILLIAN STEWART

Follow the Slope, Don't Fight it

Frequently, when you land in a bunker, you will find that you do not have a flat stance for the shot. A common bunker-play fault among handicap golfers is fighting the slope. The way to play controlled shots from such awkward places is to follow the slope.

For the downhill shot, position yourself so that the ball is in the middle of the stance with weight favouring the left side and shoulders parallel with the slope. The wrong way is ball forward and weight on the back foot.

Uphill, the ball should be quite well forward and because of the slope the weight will be naturally towards the right foot. Swing the club parallel with the slope. The wrong way is to swing into the slope.

Another problem area in bunkers is when you have to achieve a distance of 30-40 yards to the pin. For up to 20 yards, the standard technique is to open the stance and the face of the sand wedge, swinging across the ball and taking about two inches of sand behind the ball. For the longer shot, use the same stance and swing, but square up the face and hit in closer to the ball, taking about half as much sand.

● Gillian Stewart of Claremont Business Equipment, is a professional on the women's European Tour.

RIGHT . . . parallel with the slope

WRONG . . . too much weight on the right

RIGHT . . . ready to go with the slope

WRONG . . . hitting into the slope

ROBERT CRAIG

The Way to be a Splash-Hit in a Bunker

Many amateurs have a fear of bunker shots, but that can be eliminated by marrying the correct technique to plenty of practice.

When playing from a greenside bunker, always use a sand iron, and with a normal grip, ensure that both the stance and clubface are slightly open.

The ball should be positioned opposite the left heel, and wriggle the feet down into the sand. That helps to establish a firm base and test the texture of the sand (i.e. hard or soft).

Aim to hit approximately one-and-a-half inches behind the ball, and keeping the head still, swing through the sand towards the target. The ball will pop out of the bunker.

During practice, a good tip is to 'draw' a line in the sand from the ball to the left heel, and also mark the point of impact, one-and-a-half inches behind the ball. But remember, during normal play the club must not touch the sand prior to playing the shot.

When playing from a fairway bunker, the priority is to get out of the sand, so always take plenty of club. This shot differs from the greenside bunker splash shot in that the player wants to achieve maximum distance.

In order to make the desired clean hit, firm up the grip pressure, and throughout the shot, look at the top of the ball.

● **Robert Craig is the professional at Cardross.**

(Top left) Make sure the ball is opposite the left heel. (Top right) In practice ONLY, draw a line towards left heel, and mark point of impact one-and-a-half inches behind the ball in a greenside bunker. (Right) Take plenty of club from a fairway bunker, and look at the top of the ball

SHORT GAME

RONNIE MacASKILL

Accelerate into a Putt

Almost all the great putters such as Nick Faldo, Bob Charles and Tom Watson have a smooth stroke action with a long follow through. The exception is Gary Player who uses a rapping action, stopping the club after impact. That may work for him but the example of the others is better.

I have found the most common putting fault among handicap golfers is looking up too early and decelerating into the ball with the result that the ball is pushed to the right.

Position your head directly over the ball and keep the putter head as low as possible on the ground on the backswing, accelerating into the ball with a follow through twice as long as the backswing. Keep your head absolutely still and try to watch the spot the ball was sitting on.

I adopt a comfortable, narrow stance with my feet slightly open, and a reverse overlap grip (left forefinger over the right pinkie) which helps eliminate all wrist action, swinging instead from the shoulders.

Try it first on the practice green over varying lengths of putt before using it on the course where it could prevent you three-putting. Maybe you will be surprised to find yourself holing a few long ones as well!

● **Ronnie MacAskill, the professional at Royal Aberdeen, recommends Ping putters.**

Head directly over the ball, Ronnie MacAskill is in a good address position

Take the putter back low

Accelerate into the ball with a follow through twice the length of the backswing

CAMPBELL ELLIOTT

Hands, the Key to Chip Shots

Think of percentages when you are chipping from short range to a green. With a sand iron the average is 70 per cent flight and 30 per cent run. With a No. 9 iron it is 50-50, a No. 7 iron 40 per cent flight and 60 per cent run, and with a No. 5 iron the flight will be just 20 per cent. If the green is slow the run will be less and vice versa if the green is fast.

When choosing your club make sure you take enough to land the ball on the green. A common fault is landing the ball short, in which case it can bounce unpredictably.

Make sure the clubface is square to the target and choke down the grip about two inches from the top. This will give you more feel for what is basically a hands-and-arms shot. Try to feel that the pace and length of the backswing is the same as the follow through.

The most important part of this shot is to ensure that the back of the hand goes down and through towards the target, and especially that the right hand does not overtake the ball in a scooping action. The loft of the club will throw the ball into the air. The ball should be slightly further back than normal in the stance, which should be slightly open.

If the pin is positioned tightly behind a hazard, such as a bunker, you can engineer a higher percentage of flight if you can overcome the fear factor by removing the hazard from your mind.

If the lie is bare you must cut your losses, accept the 30 per cent run and play the shot as described above, but if the lie is good there is the possibility of a lob shot.

To do this take a more open stance, with the ball further forward, opposite the left heel, and open the clubface. Then employ the same technique as before — the same tempo on the backswing and through-swing, the back of the hand coming down and through towards the target.

A scooping action demonstrated by Campbell Elliott (top left) will result in a damaging shot. Instead hit down on the ball, with the back of the left hand moving towards the target (top right). The picture on the right shows clearly how the club's loft will lift the ball sharply without scooping

CAMPBELL ELLIOTT

Correct Grip Vital to Putting Success

The grip is of vital importance for putting and I would recommend the reverse overlap grip in which the left forefinger goes over the top of the fingers of the right hand. The reason is that there should be no wrist action and the grip will prevent this from happening.

Try to feel that your weight is evenly distributed, feet about shoulder width apart, and the ball just off the left heel.

The stroke is then a one-piece action. Imagine a triangle formed by the shoulder blades and down to the hands. The stroke comes from the shoulders which should work together. Remember there is no wrist action otherwise when you are under pressure you can get a flicking of the hands which will send the ball off too quickly.

The pace and length of backswing should be the same as the follow through. That will give the ball overspin which helps the ball run more truly. If you hit at the ball you can actually get damaging backspin on a putt.

For a longer putt try to feel you are swinging from inside to out which is the natural path, the one that gives the overspin. Let the putter face go across the ball to the target line. A common fault is trying to get the putter back on line by bringing the wrists into it. Remember the stroke comes from the shoulders.

The most important object of a long putt is the weight, and not the line. It is worth stating the obvious to point out that if you are six feet short and dead on line you have a more difficult putt than one that is up but two feet wide.

● Campbell Elliott, the professional at Clydebank and District, is a leading stockist of Wilson Sporting goods.

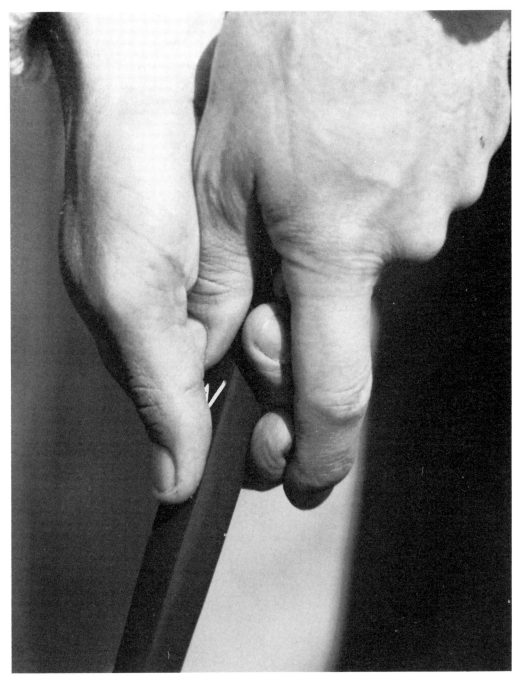

Campbell Elliott demonstrates the reverse overlap grip which eliminates wrist action in putting

KEVAN WHITSON

Wrists, the Secret of Good Putting

Putting is an area that is sadly neglected by the average club golfer and yet it is such a vital part of the game. The first priority is to find a putter with a lie and grip that makes you feel comfortable. In taking up the stance for a putt, the head should be directly over the ball. Try to imagine a line travelling straight down from your eyes through the ball.

The stroke itself should be a one-piece action, akin to a pendulum swing. There should be no movement of the wrists. And constant practice is essential to groove a consistent stroke.

Another helpful tip is one that was often advocated by Bobby Locke. If you have difficulty in judging the distance when putting, try varying the grip pressure with the thumbs — firm up for the short putts, loosen up for the long ones.

Many amateurs forget that technique in putting is just as important as for any other shot. I'm always amazed that golfers will spend hours, and hundreds of pounds, choosing woods and irons, but buy just any old putter. It is essential to have a good quality implement. After all, almost half the shots per round are played on the greens.

● Kevan Whitson is the professional at Turnhouse.

RIGHT . . . Kevan Whitson demonstrates the one-piece putting technique

WRONG . . . the wrists are broken and the pendulum movement has been lost

GARY WEIR
Secret of the Right Elbow
Handicap golfers often lose unnecessary strokes from 20-30 yards out through over anxiety. A common fault is inconsistent striking caused by the right elbow coming away from the body on the backswing and compounded by an out-to-in downswing in which the right hand is dominant. This is likely to cause the ball to be thinned or even shanked with disastrous consequences.

The cure is to concentrate on keeping your elbow tucked in on the backswing and more importantly keeping it tucked in on the downswing. This method will prevent the clubface from closing. It is also impossible to shank because the neck of the club cannot come out. Also keep your head steady and your knees comfortably flexed.

Practise this method and it could save you quite a few shots.

● **Gary Weir, the professional at Elderslie, is sponsored by Ravenstone Securities Ltd and David Le Sueur Partnership.**

WRONG . . . Gary Weir demonstrates the right elbow coming away from the body on the backswing (left) with the result (right) of a disastrous out-to-in downswing

RIGHT . . . the right elbow is tucked in on the backswing (left). Keeping it in that position on the way down is more likely to produce the desired result at impact (right)

MAUREEN GARNER

Square Up and Swing Across to Stop Quickly

A shot which frequently gives trouble is the one where you are faced with pitching over a hazard with the pin tight behind it, leaving very little green to work with. It is not necessary in this situation to open the face of the wedge, which is a difficult and specialised way of playing the shot.

Instead, try addressing the ball with the clubface square and in line with the flag (left). Adopt a narrow, slightly open stance and swing the club along the line of your feet (middle and right). That is an out-to-in path, which will impart spin on the ball, making it sit down quickly, giving you a better chance of a single putt.

● Maureen Garner, a professional on the women's European Tour, must feel right to play her best — that's why she wears Belle Golf Leisure Clothing.

JIM McCALLUM

Stay Ahead of Your Pitch Shot

The key points in short pitch shots are keep the backswing short, accelerate through the shot and hit the ball before the turf.

Many amateurs take too long a backswing which can cause a deceleration at impact. The all-too-common result is a flick shot which makes consistency in judging distance almost impossible.

For example, in a 20-yard pitch, the clubhead should not rise much above knee level (it will get slightly higher with longer shots), and in order to promote the correct action of hitting down on the ball, you must ensure that the hands stay ahead of the clubhead. In other words, lead with the hands.

It is when the ball is struck before the turf that the player generates the backspin that secures control of the shot. Guard against scooping at the ball, with the right hand passing left at impact.

There should also be very little wrist break in short pitch shots. Too steep an angle of attack results in a duffed dig shot or, alternatively, a 'thinned' effort that shoots over the green.

Also, the player should ensure he or she is comfortable at address. Keep the ball in the middle of the stance and stand slightly open with the weight favouring the left foot.

So remember — short backswing, accelerate through impact, and hit the ball, then the turf. And once you've mastered the technique — keep practising.

● Jim McCallum, professional at Lenzie, offers expert tuition, bookable in advance, free advice on equipment in his shop which is open seven days a week, and a full club repair service.

The wrong swing — it's too high

The correct way, with the club not much higher than knee level

PROBLEM SHOTS

RON WALLACE

Getting to Grips with the Rough

A common fault among club golfers is attempting over-ambitious recoveries from the rough. Frequently such efforts will result in finding even worse trouble. The first consideration must always be to reach the fairway and that means sacrificing distance. You may be able to salvage par with a pitch and single putt but if no further mistakes are made, at worst you will drop just one stroke.

That having been said, the next consideration is the grain of the grass. Playing with the grain takes less club than you would need if you were on the fairway. Swing the club normally but allow for the ball to fly higher and stronger.

A shot against the grain is much tougher. The club will be grabbed by long grass and the head will close on the ball. So open the clubface and swing the club more upright than normal to avoid catching too much grass. This technique means that the hands will stay well ahead of the clubhead at impact to keep the blade square for as long as possible. This time take more club than you would on the fairway because the rough will stop the clubhead.

● **Ron Wallace is the professional at Lanark.**

ROUGH PLAY . . . after an upright swing, Ron Wallace's hands are well through the ball just after impact to make a good recovery from an against-the-grain lie

CLIFFE JONES
Playing from Downhill and Uphill Lies

Playing from downhill and uphill lies, requires the golfer to make certain modifications to both the stance and swing. In both cases, the first rule is to align the body perpendicular to the slope.

On a downhill lie, position the ball nearer the right foot. As the shot will fade in flight, aim slightly left of target, and because the ball will fly lower off the slope take less club, for example a No. 6 iron instead of a No. 5 iron.

As there is a tendency to sway into the shot, the player should concentrate on keeping a very steady head.

On an uphill lie, everything is in reverse. Position the ball nearer the left foot, aim slightly right as the ball will draw in flight, and take one more club.

Be wary of having the ball too far forward in the stance and thereby causing the common fault of 'walking' after the ball.

With a steep, uphill lie further compensations must be made. Aim well right, take two clubs more, and bend the left knee to emphasise the lean into the slope. In order to maintain better balance, the shot should be played with just the hands and arms.

● Cliffe Jones, the professional at Glencorse, is stockist of a wide range of clubs including Taylor-Made, Karsten and Mizuno.

UPHILL . . . the ball should be forward in the stance, line up right of target and take one more club

DOWNHILL . . . position the ball nearer the right foot, aim slightly left of target and take one club less than normal for the distance

PETER THOMSON

Hands Change Can Combat Bare Lies

The result of a long, hot summer is parched courses and inevitably, tight, bare lies.

In hitting shots from such lies it is essential to keep the hands well forward both at address and throughout the shot. It is the same with every club throughout the bag, from a fairway wood to a pitching wedge.

At address, move the ball slightly back in the stance — nearer the middle of the feet — and, again it is the same for every club, try to hit the ball before the turf.

Even with the fairway woods it is impossible to sweep the ball into the air from a tight lie — hit the ball first and take a slight divot. Don't panic — fear is the amateur golfer's biggest handicap — and don't try to scoop the ball into the air.

In dry, bouncy conditions it is also unwise to attempt high chip shots as they will often kick away off line.

Take one or two clubs more than usual and play a low, running shot for the short shots to the green. I learned a great deal about these little 'feel' shots while I was serving my apprenticeship as an assistant to John Panton at Glenbervie. It is a different type of game, but the ability to play such shots is essential if you are to adapt successfully to fast running, links-type conditions.

● **Peter Thomson is the professional at Erskine where lessons and shop are available to non-members.**

A tight lie makes it impossible to sweep the ball into the air even with fairway woods as in this conventional address

Peter Thomson demonstrates the right set-up for a wood shot from such a lie — hands forward and ball in the middle of the stance

PARLIAMO GOWF

Golfspeak is a developing language. Some readers may be familiar with this kind of dialogue on the first tee prior to the Sunday morning fourball: 'We'll play a 50p Nassau with optional presses, a 5p roll-up for oozlers, 5p for ferrets, and 10p for golden ferrets and birdies.' The players nod in agreement to a statement to which any outsider, familiar with the over-used 27-hole, stroke-play European Tour format, could only say 'Eh?'.

THE GOLFERS GLOSSARY

Nassau: An agreed stake played over each of the first nine, back nine, and full round.

Press: An option by the losing player to start a fresh game at any hole.

Oozler: Nearest the pin at a par 3; if no player hits the green, the money is carried forward to the next par 3, sometimes conditional on the successful player holing in one or two putts, otherwise it becomes a foozler and the cash is forfeited.

Ferret: Holing out from off the green for par or better.

Golden Ferret: Holing out from a bunker.

Sander: Getting up and down from a bunker.

Mulligan: An option to re-take a tee shot, usually after it has been hit out of bounds, or into a hazard.

Bowff: An option to shout bowff at a time of your choosing, usually while your opponent is in the middle of a crucial shot.

Gotcha: One hesitates to go into too much detail, but on the same principle as the bowff, it is used to distract an opponent using a suitably shaped club, such as a wedge, to interfere with certain parts of his anatomy.

Chameleon: Where a player hits a wayward tee-shot on to the green of a different hole and promptly holes the putt.
Joliffe: An unusual pseudonym for a three-putt.
Otter: Any shot played into the hole from a water trap or casual water.
Chip Beck: Not the leading American golfer, but the shot you play after having hit the ball through the green (attributed to the ladies of Haggs Castle, who themselves blame the ladies of Whitecraigs because they're even more properly spoken).

● *Thanks to Colin Mackenzie of Newton Mearns for correcting and adding to the original list.*

Switch now to the clubhouse some four hours later where the four, let us call them Jim, George, Bill and Alan, are relaxing. The pints are on the table. Jim and George have won. 'Right boys, get the money out,' says Jim, in ill-founded anticipation.

Bill and Alan each sling two 50p pieces across the table for having lost the first nine by four holes, and the match by 2 and 1. Single 50p coins are returned by Jim and George in the same ungracious manner for having lost the back nine by 2 and 1, then two further contributions of the same sum for presses begun at the 7th (won 1 up) and 10th (won 2 up). Pockets continue to jingle as Bill and Alan dig for loose change to pay out 15p for one single and one double oozler, and 10p for a birdie at the 3rd. Jim and George respond with 5p for a single oozler, 20p for birdies at the 13th and 15th, the latter by virtue of a golden ferret which merits a further 25p. The transactions complete, Jim, who had been expecting a modest profit on the reasonable grounds that he had won, has the look of a bit part actor out of *The Sting* trying to figure out how the con had worked. He has actually lost 75p. More pints arrive and it is time to leave them as the conversation drifts into accusations of banditry, opinion as to where Sandy Lyle is going wrong, the latest happenings at Ibrox and Parkhead and finally an appalling jokes session.

If this seems complicated, then consider the following:

In a cross-country event at Helensburgh over the festive period, a novel twist was added. Competitors were regaled with the instructions: 'It's a four-man team event over five holes. Choose a tee shot, every team member's to be used once on the first four and the worst to be used at the 5th, each person playing the second from the selected tee shot, picking the best thereafter . . . and here's your handicap allowance.' I was handed an envelope containing a length of string and a pair of scissors. There was also a scorecard and a résumé of the rules

lest the briefing on what in effect is a modified version of the 'Texas Scramble', had not been fully understood.

Was this part of an entrance examination for Mensa? Not at all. The higher the collective handicap, the longer the length of string, which could be used to move the ball, cutting that particular length off the original measure. Most frequently the facility was used to move the ball into the hole — a perfect answer to the yips — but it could also be used to move out of bunkers, bushes, etc.

Hardly surprising, at least one string quartet got it wrong and added on a stroke every time they used the device. Nevertheless the concept lends itself to some musing over general handicap allowances.

A handicap cut could mean exactly that. Forget this variable standard scratch score system. Bulletins would be pinned to club noticeboards along the lines: 'Following a round of 64, I. Shank has had his handicap reduced by 8.5 centimetres.' The notice could then be suitably defaced with the comment: 'Get knotted.'

The idea, apparently, was inspired by an American list of novelty golf games, one other being the conversion of strokes in match-play contests into the option to order your opponent to play his shot again, under circumstances such as when he has just holed a long putt, thereby flouting one of the revered principles of golf that a player is always in control of his own ball.

Corrupt play like this is by no means new. A greensome in which a partnership chooses the better drive has from time to time been switched to a gruesome, whereby the opponents choose the worst tee shot.

There seems to be no end to the devices that are invented. Strokes have been known to be traded for Mulligans, bowffs, and, more coarsely, gotchas. Another handicapping method used without approval is the partaking of a large dram upon winning a hole (though this can lead to the contestants weaving a path down the 18th without the slightest idea of what the score is). I still feel aggrieved at a (temperant) four-ball match I played over the Ailsa course at Turnberry, no less. The stakes were a penny a yard, so that a par 3 might be worth £1.63 and a par 5 valued at £5.35. Even though we won one more hole than our opponents we had to fork out a very much grudged 35p. Golf was never meant to be a fair game!

The aforementioned 'Scramble' format is likely to become increasingly commonplace not least because Wm Teacher & Sons Ltd, sponsors of this book, are, in association with the magazine *Golf World*, laying out a £250,000 budget in 1990 in an attempt to establish the game at national level. Teams of four, open to both men and women of mixed abilities, are to compete at club level, then in area finals and a national final using the popular shotgun start.

Another popular contest at club level, and especially society outings, is the Stableford scoring system which, in 1989, was being hailed as an innovation in professional circles, having been used in the Murphy's Cup at St Pierre, Chepstow, and a modified version employed on the American Tour in the International tournament at Castle Rock, Colorado. It is, of course, a method familiar to all club golfers, but its use at the more rarified levels of the game as a welcome break from the 72-hole medal-play format, gives rise to musing that professional events for bears and sharks could be further enhanced by the games that high-handicap rabbits and minnows play. While medal play is the true game, and I am certainly not suggesting tinkering with the way majors are decided, there is surely room for a little more variety — even straight match-play is in danger of extinction.

How about a professional bogey or five-club competition, the latter perhaps helping to reduce five-hour rounds, or introducing events for teams of two — the foursome (playing alternate shots); four-ball (better ball); and greensome (selecting better drive then playing alternate shots) — or more mixed events, greatly popular at club level, but absent on the men's and women's tours.

Such is the separate nature of the two that Severiano Ballesteros and

Laura Davies, both of whom have been involved in the design of the Westerwood course near Cumbernauld, had in 1989 never met each other let alone played golf together. As far as I am aware that remains the case even though outwith the tours there are signs of merging, with the second Benson and Hedges mixed team event in Spain, and an abortive attempt to run a similar event in Holland, parallel with the Ryder Cup.

What are the merits of these various games which are frequently regarded as oddball? Under the Stableford system, invented in 1931 by Dr Frank Stableford, of the Wallasey and Royal Liverpool Club, players receive 1 point for a bogey, 2 for par, 3 for a birdie, and 4 for an eagle. Double bogey or worse earns nothing and this is the beauty of the game. Whereas in a medal, a 10 at the 1st can ruin an entire round, in Stableford the position is retrievable.

In the Murphy's Cup, an event which in 1990 is to be part of the official European Tour, this appeared to make little difference to the play, disastrous scores being far less frequent than at club level. It may be reasonable to conclude that the outcome would have been the same under medal conditions. The modified American system seems to have more to offer the professional game. Under that system no points are given for par, 2 for a birdie, and 5 for an eagle thereby encouraging an attacking approach and making the game more exciting for spectators. One point is deducted for a bogey and 3 for a double bogey or worse, giving the possibility of rapid changes on the leader board and, because up to 8 points can be made up at a single hole, a greater likelihood of keeping interest alive right to the end, a factor not necessary at club level.

The bogey competition, in which players compete against the par of individual holes, introduces a match-play element and still allows an individual to play against the entire field by the eventual tally of holes up or down against the course.

As for pairs events, this is done successfully in the professional arena of other individual sports such as tennis and snooker. In the Ryder Cup, the last of a dying breed in golf, the interest generated by such formats on the first two days, and the temperament and personality considerations that go into who plays with whom, tend to suggest it is worth a try in full four-day tournaments. What chance, for example, a harmonious Sandy Lyle/Nick Faldo pairing? And how about the prospect of a four-ball consisting of the afore-mentioned Ballesteros and Davies along with the likes of Greg Norman and Marie Laure de Lorenzi?

If the Europeans are slow in taking up novelty games, the same cannot be said of the Americans who, in 1989, held a three-day professional team event with a different format each day in the $1m Invitational Team Tournament at Thousand Oaks in California. Alternate shots was the format for the first round and a better-ball was played on the second. In the third, the scramble was used, both players hitting drives, and the best was selected as the spot from where they both hit second shots, and so on.

Then, at Daufuskie Island, South Carolina, in the Merrill Lynch Shoot-Out, the format called for ten players to start a nine-hole competition, with one player dropping out on each hole. If there is not a clear loser on each hole, the men with the highest scores play from a designated position and the man whose chip is furthest from the hole is eliminated until only two are left to play the last.

Neither must medal play be confined to the usual sum of the 18 scores less the player's handicap. A similar uplifting experience to that of Archimedes, who shouted 'Eureka' as the bathwater spilled on to the floor thereby inspiring his theory of weight displacement, may have been encountered by a certain Mr Callaway. The 'Eureka' in his case announced a handicapping system which spiked the guns of golfing bandits. Never mind the mess, he may have thought, the thing works.

The system was invented as an equitable means of awarding handicaps after the cards had been submitted, the need arising for the likes of office outings at which many players do not have official handicaps. It works thus:

A player scoring par or less keeps his tally intact. Between 1 and 5 over par, half the worst score is deducted. Between 6 and 10 over par, the whole of the worst score comes off, escalating by half a hole for every gross four shots. For example, a duffer's score of 49 over par would merit a reduction of the six worst holes. The maximum count for any hole is double the par of it and, to add spice, scores for the last two holes must stay as they are.

The conclusion seems to be that the Callaway system favours attacking play with birdies and pars rewarded, runs of bogeys and double-bogeys punished, and, unlike medal play, the occasional brainstorm forgiven. When the format was employed at Stonehaven in 1989 in a centenary competition, one player, a 20-handicapper, returned what would under normal circumstances have been a fantastic net 59, but under Callaway his score was 14 shots worse and did not even win.

It is in bounce games, however, that the real inventiveness begins as witness the glossary of terms, and in which normal etiquette is sometimes thrown out of the window and a sub-culture begins. The gimme is a case in point. Few shots in golf arouse as much emotion as the short putt — the tiddler — especially when it is not conceded by an opponent, and more so if it is then missed. If not treated with respect, the gimme can turn a round into three hours and more of psychological warfare.

How often in a 'bounce game' have you had a two-foot putt on the first green met with silence, or even heard a smirking opponent say: 'It's a long time since I've seen one of those missed.' It sets the tone for the rest of the round. Either you hole it indignantly with thoughts of levelling the score at the earliest opportunity, or worse you miss it. Friendship has, temporarily at least, flown out of the window. Your opponent is now Public Enemy No. 1.

There are subtle tactics which can be used to avert such confrontation, such as fumbling in the pocket for a marker long enough to embarrass the opposition into a *gimme* — 'Oh, for goodness sake pick it up' — or giving a putt of three feet when you have one slightly longer (a gambit liable to backfire). It all boils down to gamesmanship. State of mind is all-important when dealing with *that* length of putt. When it does not matter it is simple to knock it in holding the putter with one hand and sometimes with the wrong side of the blade. When it does matter the muscles tense and negative thoughts prevail. An appalling jab is frequently the result, but let's leave the yips for another occasion.

The point here is that golf is one of the few sports in which concessions can be given. In tennis the player at the net still has to stroke the ball over the other side to make the point, in football the striker must tap the ball over the goal-line to score, and in snooker the black hanging over the pocket must be put away. There is no room for give and take. Those of a miserable disposition will point to famous missed putts. Well, would you have given Doug Sanders that curling four-footer to win the Open at St Andrews in 1970, or Craig Stadler the tiddler he missed at The Belfry in 1985 which swung the Ryder Cup in Europe's favour? You would almost certainly, however, have given Hale Irwin that putt of no more than a few inches at the Open at Birkdale which he fresh-aired when attempting to tap-in in 1983 and finished one stroke behind Tom Watson. It just goes to show how generosity can often be misplaced.

Certainly, the significance of giving three-footers grows as the round progresses. You may concede one with gay abandon at the 1st, but not at the 18th where 50p may be at stake. Not quite in the league of Curtis Strange's $135,000 for a single hole in the Skins Game in California in 1989, but exactly the same in principle.

So am I advocating a policy of holing-out at all times, as is the case in some hard-line Club Golf schools? Not at all. Consider the case of possibly the most famous *gimme* in the history of the game.

When Jack Nicklaus gave Tony Jacklin that little tester at Birkdale in 1969 which resulted in Britain and Ireland tying for the Ryder Cup, the American said: 'I don't think you would have missed that but I'm not going to give you the chance.' It may have cost America an outright win, as some of Nicklaus's team-mates pointed out, but it was one of those supreme acts of sportsmanship which will be recounted through the ages. Timely given putts can make friends for life, but it doesn't mean that a few wind-ups cannot be had along the way. 'I'll see that one in, thank you.'

The vernacular is important in such games, and terms have been collated by county golf official Jim Muldrew of B. J. Aitken Builders of Glasgow to hand out to golfing clients. Herewith a selected 25 in A-Z format:

Air-mailed it: a shot over the green
Back stalls: back tees
Cabbage pounder: lot of time in the rough
Dutch Harrison: reputation as a needler
Enough stick: correct club selection
Feather it in: delicate pitch or wedge
Gonzo: ball lost
H2O'd: in the water
In the throw-up zone: six-foot putt
Jack it up: preferred lie
Kick-in distance: short putt
Let the big dog eat: plan to hit a long drive
Mr Aerosol: golfer who sprays his shots
Noodled it: curved recovery shot out of woods
On the dance floor: on the green in regulation
Put my nails on: put on golf shoes
Quail high: low shot
Recovery room: clubhouse
Stretcher bearers: caddies
Taxi: cry of anguish as a putt slides past the hole
Up and down out of the ball-washer: skilful around the green
Van Gogh it: an artistic shot around the green
Worm-burner: a poor, ground-hugging shot
Yank: duck hook
Zeppelin: skied ball

The omission of a term for the letter X suggests in all probability that there is not one, although Dr John McMinn of North Berwick uses a literary leather mashie to get one into his own little ditty, which he has used in the past as a turn at golf club functions as follows:

A   for the address, standing silent in prayer,
     that after your shot, the ball won't still be there.
B   is for bunker, by sand you're surrounded,
     only the teeth, not the club, may be grounded.
C   is for Council, who, while asserting their status,
     at meetings pass ultra-high frequency flatus.
D   is for divot, a sod flying through space,
     then the sod or his partner must that divot replace.
E   is for eagle, as rare as the bird,
     when I've had two more, then my next is my third.
F   is for 'FORE!' warning 'Duck, or I'll hit ye',
     it's a MUST before felling one of the Committee.

G is for gamesmanship, it's not the done thing,
    to drop clubs at the top of an opponent's backswing.
H is for hazard, which may cost you a shot, or
    you may pee on your ball, and claim 'casual water'.
I   is for ignorance, of which I've a lot,
    combined with brute force, it takes yards off my shot.
J   is for Jesus, whose advice is much sought,
    in an advisory capacity, after a shot.
K is for knickers, which are apt to get twisted,
    when you've a putt, for the match, on the 18th, and missed it.
L   is the love for our golf, and our wives,
    and the second comes first if we value our lives.
M for machines that stand in the hall,
    and pay out a percentage of $pi\ r^2$ damn all.
N for the nineteenth, where, with spirits imbued,
    each member displaces his own volume of fluid.
O for the orifice, so round and so small,
    into which which I cannot put the ball.
P   is for par, a score almost mythical,
    can I score par figures? Oh! Get on your bythical.
Q for queer notices you can find yourself facin',
    such as: 'Members must NOT wash their balls in the basin.'
R is for reading, a green, not a tome,
    but some are slow readers, and should take the green home.
S   for the shakes that come on when we putt,
    indicating the alcohol intake be cut.
T   for tall tales of scores under par,
    my friends always play their best shots in the bar.
U for umbilicus, sometimes called belly button,
    it steadies the shaft of my club when I'm putting.
V is for V sign made with two upright fingers,
    when opponent's ball runs to the hole, then lingers.
W is for women, who I have not found,
    willing to join me in playing around.
X Xpert advice on my golf never varies,
    it's: 'Gie the gemme up Jack! Ye're away wi' the fairies.'
Y is the yen for the yon, which we seek,
    if you've no yen for yon, then you're right up the creek.
Z is your zenith, your swansong, euphoria,
    keep taking the tablets, chum, for *sic transit gloria*.

JOHN McMINN

A CHANCE IN TEN MILLION BILLION

Winning the Open championship is every club golfer's dream. Who can fail to fantasise, while striding over the Swilken Bridge on the 18th at St Andrews, that he needs a par 4 to get his name on that silver claret jug? The message here is keep on hoping because it *is* a possibility for all golfers with a handicap of 10 or better. Extremely remote certainly, but theoretically possible according to the experience of the first two years of examining medal scores in the *Glasgow Herald*'s Tuesday Club Golf page.

Weekly competition returns in peak summer have thrown up winners with scores of 10 under their handicap and more — 17-under was reached one week. This represents gross scoring, for 10-handicappers and better, akin to that which would be expected of an Open champion, and can be regarded as the best score from an estimated field of 10,000. Now brace yourself for an appalling statistical calculation.

If such a phenomenal score is a 10,000 to one shot, it follows that the chances of producing four such rounds in a row, which an Open champion would be required to do, is 10,000 multiplied by itself four times. That works out at one in 10,000,000,000,000,000, or one in ten million billion. It would probably be comparable with winning the pools jackpot two weeks in a row. But remember you have that chance! All we have to do is persuade the Royal and Ancient Golf Club of St Andrews to introduce a means of allowing 10-handicap golfers to qualify for the Open. Either that or lie about your handicap on the entry form like Maurice 'The Menace' Flitcroft — remember, he was the one who slipped through the net and played his first full 18-holes in an Open qualifying round and managed only one par in a round of 121 dreadful shots.

There are ways of reducing the odds, such as practising (perish the thought), or better still by creating a more ambitious environment for juniors to improve, a subject which will be looked at later in the book. In the meantime, however, we will concentrate on the concept of an ordinary club golfer's round of a lifetime. The beauty about what has happened here is that it could have been you or I who did it. We don't need outrageous odds to tell us what we can really do if we play to our capabilities.

The almost defamatory Bandit-of-the-Week title is conferred upon the player who breaks his (or her) handicap by the most. Interestingly, no one has complained, at least not to us, about such a designation. Moreover, when interviewed, the culprits, virtually without exception, have said the same thing: 'It was just one of those rounds.' What that has meant in effect is that every shot was played to expectation. There was no sudden discovery of an extra 50 yards off the tee, no lucky leprechaun bouncing out of the woods and offering the secret of golf, nothing spectacular. It has been a case of disaster avoidance, no 3-putts and the occasional long one sunk, no brainstorms in bunkers or in the rough, and no duffs.

Our bandits, in short, are nothing of the kind though one or two — and by no means all — through no fault of their own, have perhaps been given handicaps higher than they ought to have been. Analyses have shown that in a field of 100 a score of 5-under is usually needed to win. Extending that to 10,000, scores of 10-under and more are not out of place in statistical terms even if, at club level, the perpetrator is painted as a desperado.

Any self-respecting, handicap-protecting hustler of the fairways would never dream of drawing attention to himself or herself by coming in with the kind of score guaranteed to send the club handicap secretary to the bar for a heavy anaesthetic. Win quietly, maybe 2 or 3 under handicap, is their motto, not least because that way their handicap will have a slight but insignificant change. Our bandits have had their handicaps savaged under the notorious Clause 19 by up to 7 shots in one fell swoop. Consequently, and also perhaps as a result of the heavy odds against repeating such a round, none of our top bandits beat their handicap when we invited them to our shoot-out, the Parbusters final at Haggs Castle, more of which later. First let's have a look at a few case examples.

The first bandit, and the one who set the fascinating trend, was Archie Gibb, a 9-handicapper at Paisley, who returned a 72, level with the day's competition scratch score. In other words he beat his handicap by 9. A former centre-forward with amateur side Paisley Spartans, he had been playing golf for less than three years — a late starter at the age of 30. A full statistical analysis, a common trait

Myra Davidson

among golfers, was provided, presumably aided by his professional
accountancy skills. He missed only one fairway and just four greens in
regulation compared to his average of four and 12 respectively for all of
the previous season. He had 32 putts, three bogeys and two birdies, the
balance against par being made up by the increase of 1 in the CSS.

What was the secret? 'I don't know,' he said. 'It was just one of
those rounds when everything went right.' It is a quote which, in club
golfing circles, has become as platitudinous, if essentially as justified, as
the football manager's 'the boys done good' and 'we are taking one
game at a time'.

Next was a woman, Myra Davidson, who returned a net 12-under-
par 58 off a handicap of 30 over the Barrhead club of Fereneze.

99

'Everything went right. There was nothing spectacular, no long putts holed, but I never got into trouble.' Trouble avoidance was to become a consistent theme. Myra and then 26-handicap husband Dan were shortly to move to Livingston to a house *on* a golf complex. We figured, especially as Myra was still a 24-handicapper, that this would not be the last we would hear of the Davidsons, and we were right, though not quite in the way expected. Almost a year to the day we heard from Deer Park about a case of 'anything Mum can do, I can do better'. Myra's 15-year-old son, Campbell, carded over Deer Park a net 57 in a junior medal, 15-under-par off a handicap of 31. The next week he shot a net 58 off 25, and was duly cut to 16 — a reduction of 15 in eight days. In an amazing twist, Campbell's clubs were the same ones Mum used to bring Fereneze to its knees. They must have been touched by that lucky leprechaun after all, although Myra's score was eventually beaten by Anne Stewart of Irvine Kidsneuk, who beat her 23 handicap by 14 shots in a competition over Caprington.

The footballer-turned-golfer trend continued with Ayr Belleisle's Jim Tierney, who played wing and midfield for Bradford City, Irish side Portadown, and finally Ayr United, which made him an honest man and a bandit at the same time. He shot a round of gross 3 under the CSS — off a handicap of 6 despite taking a bogey 6 at the last in near pitch darkness.

We have yet to hear of a net score in the 40s, but we would have done if banker John Hamilton, a 25-handicapper of Cathcart Castle, had not blown up over the last four holes over which he tallied 6, 6, 5, 7 but still managed to card a net 54, which beat his handicap by no fewer than 14 shots. The same feat was achieved by veterinary surgeon David Snodgrass, who caused his 2-handicap marker at Dunbar a sharp intake of breath when, after a round of 75, he disclosed that his handicap was 18. 'My partner, who scored the same as myself, thought I had a similar handicap. He was astonished.'

Breaking 100 for the first time is a milestone in every golfer's career, and 15-year-old Susan McLaughlin of Cardross combined that with becoming a weekly bandit. Her score of 99 less 33 gave her a net score of 9 under the course's par of 75, and returning to the subject of 10-handicappers, Margie Ross, a 19-year-old student of maths and psychology (fine credentials for a golfer), earned the course record at Ralston with a score of 73, 1 over par, despite 3-putting the 17th. Course records have also been equalled or beaten by unexpectedly high handicappers in John Munro, who equalled the Aberfeldy record of 66 — then deducted his handicap of 11, and 6-handicapper Ian MacFarlane, who shot a gross 4-under-par 62 over Bridge of Allan to reduce the previous record by one.

The entire field in the 1988 August medal at Royal Aberdeen could collectively have been termed bandits — 28 players had their handicaps cut, chiefly Bill Hay, an optician, and clubmates could hardly believe their eyes when he counted up his score and tallied 78 — less his handicap of 21. 'It was just one of those days when everything went right,' he said, and he was neither the first nor last to say that. And the round, once again, was almost disaster-free — with the exception of a lost ball at the 5th, by no means calamitous off such a high handicap.

Scott Ramage, a 27-year-old 24-handicapper — and a former footballer — ran up, not for the first time, a 7 at the 1st over Kirkhill. Some three hours later after a round played in wet, windy conditions, he canned an eight-footer at the last for a net 58, to beat his handicap by 12, then said: 'Everything went right on the day after the first' (now where have we heard that before?), 'particularly my putting, which is often erratic. There were no birdies, but lots of pars.' At the end of the first year, the overall table stood:

HANDICAP

Men

J. Hamilton, Cathcart Castle (25) ....-14
D. R. Snodgrass, Dunbar (18) ....-14
B. Hay, Royal Aberdeen (21) ....-13
J. Spence, Loudoun (16) ....-13
H. Howie, West Kilbride (17) ....-12
A. Gemmill, Ralston (22) ....-12
J. Munro, Aberfeldy (11) ....-12
S. Ramage, Kirkhill (24) ....-12
C. Marshall, Cawder (22) ....-11
D. L. Dunbar, Williamwood (25) ....-11
J. Edgar, Hamilton (25) ....-11
G. M. Grant, Glasgow (16) ....-11
B. McMillan, Eastwood (21) ....-11

Women

A. Stewart, Irvine Kidsneuk, over Caprington (23) ....-14
M. Davidson, Fereneze (30) ....-12
L. Paton, Clydebank & District (28) ....-12
E. McGrath, Cawder (36) ....-11
R. Grant, Strathaven (25) ....-11
R. Peebles, Haggs Castle (22) ....-10
M. Miller, Windyhill (25) ....-10
S. McKenzie, Ranfurly Castle (27) ....-10
S. Sheret, Palacerigg (36) ....-10
R. Robb, East Kilbride (18) ....-10
H. Steele, Dumfries & County (20) ....-10

SCRATCH

Men

S. Inglis, Falkirk	-6
C. Ronald, Torrance House	-6
G. Wilson, Palacerigg	-5
A. Hannah, Hamilton	-5
W. Bryson, Colville Park	-5
A. C. N. Fleming, Whitecraigs	-4
D. MacAndrew, Royal Aberdeen	-4
I. Mackenzie, Haggs Castle	-4
J. I. McCosh, Cochrane Castle	-4
D. Tierney, Ayr Belleisle	-4
B. S. Yuill, Douglas Park	-4
I. A. Carslaw, Western Gailes	-4
B. Kerr, Biggar	-4
D. J. Barbour, Cathkin Braes	-4
B. M. Gossman, West Kilbride	-4

Women

J. Kinloch, Cardross	-3
A. Prentice, Bothwell Castle	-1
S. McMahon, Cardross	-1
A. Henderson, Milngavie	-1
A. Rose, Stirling	level
M. Mulligan, Strathaven	level
S. Piewak, Dunbar	level

The exercise so far had been partly experimental and it was regrettable that by the time a tournament was seriously thought about, it was too late to get these players together. However, small prizes were sent out to the top ten in each section and efforts began in earnest to prepare for 1989.

In May the search began for the four *Glasgow Herald* club golfers of the year, men's and women's scratch and handicap. Wm Teacher & Son were by now in on the act by giving bottles of Teacher's Highland Cream to weekly section winners, along with the *Herald*'s contribution of six balls. The cumulative top ten in each section were to be invited to compete in a shoot-out final at Haggs Castle.

First on the scene was Eric Keltie, a 54-year-old self-employed painter and decorator with a handicap of 21, who carded a net 59 over Troon St Meddans in a medal over the Darley course. Rangers Football Club had a hand in it. 'I used to be a die-hard, but Rangers were on the way down about six years ago and I took up golf instead,' he said, showing some remorse by adding: 'But I am sorry I packed up when I did. It was the wrong time to quit just when Graeme Souness came on the scene although this score makes me feel that at least I did something right.'

Shortly after came the most fantastic score yet by Alex McVey, a 37-year-old physical education teacher. It was probably the case that his handicap, through no fault of his own, was too high at 26. Yet that was the mark which his initial cards merited. This in itself is a case in point for never awarding first handicaps higher than 18, with the option of raising it after a year.

Alex, yet another former footballer, having played at junior level with Ashfield and Pollock, practised over the winter (how many people do that?), and as a result was entitled to expect an improvement though perhaps not as much as really happened in the Cawder Spring Meeting. Over the flat Keir Course, which, with little trouble is considered a fairly soft option compared to the neighbouring Cawder Course which is nicknamed 'Vietnam', he took four shots to reach the par 4 first green, which is easily reached with a drive and a pitch. Then he holed a 30-footer for bogey and never looked back, hitting a hot patch from the 14th from where he went birdie, par, birdie, before finishing cautiously for a 77 less 26 — 17 under his handicap. That is a mark which has yet to be beaten in the banditry stakes, but unfortunately Alex could not get the time off to try and show his mettle in our final.

Meanwhile, the course records continued to tumble under unexpected circumstances. Gillian Brodie, wife of the former Scottish amateur champion and Walker Cup player Allan, went round Lenzie in a record 72, 3 over the SSS — even though she was five months pregnant. If only for the benefit of male chauvinist golfers who never think about such a matter, let alone experience it (with the exception perhaps of trying to swing round an expanding midriff), Gillian offered some explanation. 'I needed no adjustment — I'm not really that big yet. In fact, I'm not really feeling pregnant,' she said, vowing to carry on playing for as long as possible. It was a measure of the way Parbusters was progressing that this feat did not even merit a prize — there were three better scores that week.

At Falkirk Tryst, Pamela Laird, a 32-handicapper, went round in 15 below her mark. The unusual thing about this, apart from her score, was that it was in a five-club competition, her selection a driver, No. 5 wood, No. 7 iron, wedge, and putter. 'There was no spectacular scoring, but I had nothing worse than a 6 on my card,' she said, confirming a by now well-established pattern and prompting her husband, who had bought her a full set of clubs for Christmas, to threaten to return the remainder and ask for a refund. He was joking — we think!

In the scratch stakes, Gary Blair of Troon Welbeck, ran up a Darley course record of 65, 7 under the CSS and the best scratch score thus far, despite driving out of bounds at the par-5 9th and holing only one long putt. He countered with nine birdies, all from close-range putts. 'It wasn't bad,' he said with classic understatement. Similarly, Ken Goodwin shot a course-record 65, 5 under the CSS over Glenbervie, then said: 'I didn't really play that well,' explaining that he hit only six fairways off the tee, but made five birdies from them and scrambled elsewhere. In the same week Suzanne Mailer of Auchterarder recorded a record 65 over Callander.

At Golspie, Jennifer MacKenzie became the second woman to become a weekly bandit by breaking 100 for the first time. In fact she shot a 95 — 14 less than her previous best — less 36 to beat her handicap by 12. 'I usually have a couple of 10s, but this time I was never in trouble. I didn't go into the rough, missed bunkers, and the putts went in for a change,' she said, again confirming the requirements for the round of a lifetime.

You might imagine offshore on the oil rigs to be a golfing desert, but 23-handicapper Ian Ward of Hilton Park disproved this theory by coming in with a net 59 after two weeks on BP's Thistle Alpha in the North Sea whence it is a 150-mile carry to the Shetland Isles. Hitting balls from the rig is frowned upon, especially by divers, but Ian said: 'Harry Bannerman was out here a while ago to give lessons, and he was given permission to launch a few into the water, but otherwise we have a driving net outdoors beside the helipad. It is useful for practising lessons from our golf videos. The Jack Nicklaus and latest Peter Alliss ones are quite good,' he said. Clearly if you are a golf nut you will find the means to play in even the most hostile environment. That week comedian Andy Cameron was one of 24 players who beat their handicap by 7 but did not merit even a mention in listings because there were so many on 8-under and better.

Course records were beaten in the same week at Largs and Gullane No. 3 by Charles White (5 under CSS 64) and David Kirkpatrick (4 under CSS 61), neither of whom won even the competition they were playing in, handicappers having come in with lower net scores. That was far from the case for Andrew McKee of Stranraer, who became the first winner of both scratch and handicap sections with a 70, 4 below the CSS, and 11 below it after his handicap of 7 was deducted. It was in the club championship and he was pipped by 1 for the title because of an 82 in the first round. 'I had the choice of being scratch runner-up or outright winner in the handicap section. I decided on the latter because the trophy went with it,' he said, lamenting his opening round. His achievement of winning both sections was followed by Stewart Shaw, a 21-year-old broker of Kirkintilloch with a gross 61 and net 55 which was 11 below his handicap, and Brian Campbell, a 29-year-old computer assembler of Gourock, a 9-handicapper, who shot a gross 70, 4 under the CSS.

Nicky Balic, a 25-year-old painter and decorator from Greenburn, West Lothian, beat his 19 handicap by 12 shots without a wooden club in his bag, while at the other end of the age scale senior citizen Betty Philip from Crieff, 18 months after a hip operation, carded an 11-under-par 63 off a handicap of 27. 'It was a joy to hit the ball so well again,' she said. The final at Haggs loomed and the qualifiers were:

HANDICAP

Men
A. McVey, Cawder (26) .... -17
T. Paul, Greenock (25) .... -13
B. Campbell, Gourock (9) .... -13
E. Keltie, Troon St Meddans (21) .... -12
E. Bruce, Old Ranfurly (26) .... -12
A. Stewart, Easter Moffat (27) .... -12
J. Orr, Castle Douglas (22) .... -12
G. Spalding, Falkirk (21) .... -12
N. Balic, Greenburn (19) .... -12
J. Shanks, Airdrie (17) .... -12

The seven on -12 were balloted from nine. Others on the same score were J. Keddie, Southerness (23); J. MacDonald, Cawder (14).

Women
P. Laird, Falkirk Tryst (32) .... -15
N. Chalmers, Torrance House (27) .... -13
J. Stark, Lochwinnoch (34) .... -12
I. Carr, Powfoot (29) .... -12
J. MacKenzie, Golspie (36) .... -12
H. Guthrie, Troon Welbeck (36) .... -11
B. Philip, Crieff (27) .... -11
J. Holmes, Calderbraes (28) .... -11
M. Chapman, Calderbraes (29) .... -11
G. Gallagher, Bonnybridge (30) .... -11

The five on -11 were balloted from 11. Others on the same score were: R. Cowan, Gourock (34); W. Askew, Colville Park (26); F. Scott, Cathcart Castle (21); D. Steele, Elie and Earlsferry (28); P. Smith, Dumfries & Galloway (25); A. Lyden, Greenock (25).

Parbusters winners 1989

SCRATCH

Men

G. Blair, Troon Welbeck	-7
C. Ronald, Torrance House	-6
C. Barrowman, Jr., Clydebank & District	-5
K. W. Goodwin, Glenbervie	-5
C. White, Largs	-5
F. Stewart, Prestonfield	-5
S. Shaw, Kirkintilloch	-5
D. Kirkpatrick, Gullane	-4
W. Moore, Jr., Ravenspark	-4
J. A. Currie, East Kilbride	-4

The three on -4 were balloted from nine. Others on the same score were: H. Bonnacorsi, Stranraer; A. McKee, Stranraer; D. S. Gray, Ranfurly Castle; B. Campbell, Gourock; S. A. Campbell, Machrihanish; P. Semple, Clydebank Overtoun.

Women

M. Hughes, Wishaw	-4
S. Mailer, Auchterarder	-3

J. Kinloch, Cardross .... -3
D. Jackson, Cochrane Castle .... -3
J. Gardner, Haggs Castle .... -2
J. Risby, Bishopbriggs .... -1
I. C. Robertson, Troon .... -1
L. Anderson, Cawder .... -1
L. Jamieson, Crieff .... -1
A. Rose, Stirling .... level

The score on level par was balloted from four. Others on the same score were: A. Prentice, Bothwell Castle; M. Wilson, Turnberry; L. Lundie, Strathaven.

After reserves were called in the final line-up was as follows, and it was interesting to note that the average handicap reduction of the women taking part was 8, Pamela Laird showing the biggest reduction by falling from 32 to 19, while the men's average was 5.2, Andrew Stewart of Easter Moffat topping the excellence stakes with a drop from 27 to 17.

*Figures show extent of handicap reduction since Parbusters qualifying scores were posted.

Women — Pamela Laird (Falkirk Tryst) 32-19; Nance Chalmers (Torrance House) 27-19; Janette Stark (Lochwinnoch) 34-26; Isabelle Carr (Powfoot) 29-23; Jennifer MacKenzie (Golspie) 36-27; Helen Guthrie (Troon Welbeck) 36-24; Betty Phillip (Crieff) 27-19; Jessie Holmes (Calderbraes) 28-20; Margaret Chapman (Calderbraes) 29-23; Gwen Gallagher (Bonnybridge) 30-22

Men — Tom Paul (Greenock) 25-20; Brian Campbell (Gourock) 9-6; Eric Keltie (Troon St Meddans) 21-17; Eddie Bruce (Old Ranfurly) 26-20; Andrew Stewart (Easter Moffat) 27-17; John Orr (Castle Douglas) 22-18; George Spalding (Falkirk) 21-16; Nicholas Balic (Greenburn) 19-15; John Shanks (Airdrie) 17-14

The tournament itself was not without incident, and one thing that will be tidied up in 1990 will be the official use of the variable standard scratch score system. We were unaware that the permission of the Scottish Golf Union was required to make it a counting event for handicap purposes, and therefore the scores calculated by this method are of interest only, although very much in keeping with the way Parbusters had been presented. Here's what happened:

MEN: SSS 71, CSS 73. WOMEN: SSS 73.

HANDICAP

Men

Nicholas Balic, Greenburn (15)	+ 1
John Orr, Castle Douglas (18)	+ 5
Brian Campbell, Gourock (6) bih	+ 7
Eddie Bruce, Old Ranfurly (20) bih	+ 7
John Shanks, Airdrie (14)	+ 7
Eric Keltie, Troon St Meddans (17)	+ 9
Tom Paul, Greenock (20)	+ 10
Andrew Stewart, Easter Moffat (17)	+ 11
George Spalding, Falkirk (16)	+ 15

Women

Isabelle Carr, Powfoot (23)	+ 5
Gwen Gallacher, Bonnybridge (22)	+ 7
Nance Chalmers, Torrance House (19)	+ 9
Janette Stark, Lochwinnoch (26)	+ 13
Pamela Laird, Falkirk Tryst (19)	+ 15
Betty Philip, Crieff (19) bih	+ 16
Helen Guthrie, Troon Welbeck (24)	+ 16
Jennifer MacKenzie, Golspie (27)	+ 18
Jessie Holmes, Calderbraes (20)	+ 21
Margaret Chapman, Calderbraes (23)	+ 23

SCRATCH

Men

Craig Ronald, Torrance House	-2
William Moore, Ravenspark	+ 1
Charles White, Largs	+ 2
Stewart Shaw, Kirkintilloch bih	+ 4
Fraser Stewart, Prestonfield bih	+ 4
Cliff Barrowman, Clydebank & District bl6	+ 4
Derek Gray, Ranfurly Castle	+ 4
Paul Semple, Clydebank Overtoun	+ 5
Andrew McKee, Stranraer	+ 10

Women

Alison Rose, Stirling	+ 1
Lorna Lundie, Strathaven	+ 4
Lorna Bennett, Ladybank bih	+ 5
May Hughes, Wishaw	+ 5
Janice Risby, Bishopbriggs bih	+ 6
Donna Jackson, Cochrane Castle bih	+ 6
Lindsey Anderson, Cawder	+ 6
Suzanne Mailer, Auchterarder	+ 9
Janice Gardner, Haggs Castle	+ 10

The first *Glasgow Herald* Parbusters tournament run in association with Wm Teacher & Sons turned out to be the day the bandits left their ammunition at home, the scratch players excelled, and the Club Golf page found its very own Supergran in the form of 74-year-old Isabelle Carr, who became a champion despite finding herself trapped between two locked doors in mid-round.

Not one player broke his or her mark in the handicap sections despite near-perfect conditions at Haggs Castle, suggesting that the qualifying scores of 11-under or better were all one-offs and that match secretaries have succeeded in doing effective hatchet jobs. A measure of the overall performance was that the competition scratch score was 73, a rise of 2 from the SSS. In fact, the best handicap score, a net 68, was produced by 5-handicapper Andy Aitken of Stirling, winner of the match secretary of the year award, who was then required to wield the axe on himself. Among the guests, 4-handicapper David Sergeant of Bishopbriggs beat his handicap by 1 with a great round.

The best story — if not the best golf — came in the women's handicap section. In the shotgun start, Isabelle, the 23-handicapper from Powfoot, who has three children and seven grandchildren, began at the 9th and by the time she came off the 18th green she was in need of a visit to the powder room.

'On the way out I saw a door halfway down the stairs leading into the car park but found it was locked. Then when I turned round I realised the door behind me had closed and locked itself. I was stuck.'

No one could hear Isabelle pounding the doors and shouting as her playing partners, Lorna Lundie and Paul Semple, waited patiently on the first tee. A case, you might say, of oh dear what can the matter be?

Meanwhile a passer-by heard the cries for help and came to the rescue. 'I was trapped for 15 minutes and it seemed like an hour,' she laughed afterwards.

But Isabelle is made of stern stuff and although she took a 9 at the par-5 4th (her 14th) after bunker trouble, she steadied herself to finish with a net 78 and victory by two shots from Gwen Gallacher of Bonnybridge.

'The tournament was a lovely idea, we were all treated very well, and I think it was a great success,' she added.

The best scratch score, a 71 which was 2 under the CSS, was carded by 19-year-old plus-2-handicapper Craig Ronald of Torrance House, a former Scottish boys' and youths' cap with a round starting at the first which featured birdies at the 9th, 16th and 18th.

In the women's scratch section, 21-year-old Alison Rose, the East of Scotland women's champion and a semi-finalist that year in the Scottish Women's Championship, made it a Stirling double in recovering from a 7 at the par-4 13th (her sixth) to finish on 74, the best women's score of the day. After her disaster caused by hitting out of bounds, she recovered with an eagle 3 at the next and completed the remaining 11 holes in 2 under par.

There was a special prize for Janice Risby of Bishopbriggs, who recovered from an outward 45 with an inward 34 featuring three birdies.

Nicky Balic, a 15-handicapper from Greenburn, took the men's handicap award, finishing 1 over the CSS despite having carded three treble bogeys. The 25-year-old self-employed painter and decorator had seven pars elsewhere to finish 1 over his handicap.

The top three in the handicap and scratch sections each won PGA vouchers and bottles of Teacher's Highland Cream whisky, a half-gallon going to each winner along with an engraved crystal trophy.

A remarkable fact is that every competitor returned a score, no matter how bad. There is honour in that, and it was fun, which was the main objective.

Our man with the shotgun, David Begg, the tournament director, has officiated as press officer for the Open Championship, Ryder Cup, and Dunhill Cup. To that impressive list he can now add Parbusters and there is a tenuous link.

A delve into the archives reveals that the last time the *Glasgow Herald* was involved in running a tournament it evolved into the Ryder Cup. The year was 1920, venue Gleneagles, and titled the *Glasgow Herald* 1000 Guineas Tournament, it was contested by the leading players of America and Great Britain.

Today Parbusters, tomorrow who knows what? At least there is a willingness by all those involved to repeat the exercise.

Running in tandem was a competition for match secretaries, who had had the task of sending in the competition returns throughout the year, and who were drawn, two every month, to receive prizes and places in our tournament. That resulted:

Andy Aitken, Stirling	-5
Mary Borland, Old Ranfurly (17)	+ 1
John McQueen, Kilbirnie Place (12)	+ 6
Ken McLauchlan, Millport (11)	+ 7
Frank Gilmour, Largs (9)	+ 8
Kathleen Sinclair, Elderslie (14)	+ 10
Jay Lamsdell, Forres (14)	+ 15

SPOILED FOR CHOICE

If all the golf holes in Scotland were laid end-to-end they would stretch about 1,000 miles and fit in an enormous meandering line between John O' Groats and Land's End; and if the 420 courses were joined together into one, the excruciating statistics would be in the region of a 7,000-hole 1,900,000-yard par 25,000.

Royal Scotland, as we might call this hypothetical eighth wonder of the world, could be negotiated on a 36-holes-a-day basis in just over six months but has anyone played every course in Scotland? Mountaineers have often done so in their particular sphere of obsession — climbing Munros — but I have never heard of the equivalent golfing achievement.

There is, perhaps, a good reason for this. It never seems satisfactory to play a course once. The first time, invariably through playing badly, can always be put down to reconnaissance. The performance, you feel, will be better second, third or fourth time round, *ad infinitum*.

Checking through listings in the *Golfer's Handbook*, I discovered that my personal tally is 70, in some respects a humbling total because it means there are 350 courses I have not played. I suspect that few golfers reach a total of even 100, largely, perhaps, through loyalty to their own club. I am sure that I have played more rounds over Helensburgh, my regular place of worship, than all others put together. Surely it would take an extremely single-minded golfer to achieve a full house.

Another pointless but thought-provoking exercise is to select personal favourite holes and put them together into a course. These holes may not have any great aesthetic quality but are picked because I have felt a buzz of excitement on the tee. My choice, restricted to no

111

more than one hole per course, shows a penchant for elevated tees. There may be a Freudian explanation for this but, on a more practical plane, the course would drop from start to finish by several hundred feet and might therefore require a chairlift to the first tee.

I have 'constructed' only a nine-hole course, a 3,517-yard par 37, leaving scope for extending to 18 holes in the future.

1.   Cottage: Williamwood. 13th. 254-yard par 4

Only just par 4, this hole has a splendidly elevated tee inviting you to have a go. Just the sort of start to get the adrenalin pumping. The green is reachable with a good wallop — tremendously satisfying if achieved.

2.   Tinkler's Gill: Gleneagles, Queens. 12th. 407-yard par 4

There is an obvious target here for the tee shot — a steep downhill slope at just beyond 200 yards. All but the faint-hearted will be tempted to have a go at making it. Failure will still leave you an interesting long second to the green way below.

3.   Braid's Bend: Cardross. 16th. 490-yard par 5

A dog-leg right defined by high trees. In serious play it might be rash to go for anything other than position off the tee. In a bounce game, however, it is irresistible to try and cut the corner with a high fade. My own efforts have usually ended crashing into the trees, but success is unforgettable, turning the hole into a realistic par 4.

4.   Ben Bouie: Helensburgh. 4th. 372-yard par 4

A long drive down two slopes will leave a short pitch over a three-in-one bunker known as 'Jaws'. In dry conditions you must land the ball on the upslope fringe otherwise it is likely to go bounding through the back. A wayward drive still leaves the possibility of par although the approach must be exact to the heavily-guarded green.

5.   Dardanelles: Stornoway. 11th. 547-yard par 5

A double dog-leg downhill, then uphill through a wooded neck, and downhill again. The hole is an exercise in restraint. A good drive may tempt you to cut corners but beware. A medium-iron second is more advisable, leaving a long third. That way you may finish with a 6 but at least you will have avoided double figures.

6.   Muckle Drap: Hilton Park. 17th. 182-yard par 3

Some light relief from the rigours of the last hole. You will get a crick in your neck looking down at this green. The shot can range from a No. 8 iron to a full wood depending on the wind. The excitement mounts as the ball plummets to reveal whether you have selected the right club.

7.   Kelvin: Cawder. 14th. 454-yard par 4

Another elevated tee, but not one to be treated with abandon. Out of bounds on the left, and water and trees on the right will give you much distraction. A big drive, however, will open up the green for a long second over more water.

8. Bruce's Castle: Turnberry, Ailsa. 9th. 455-yard par 4

The championship tee, if you ever have the opportunity to play from it, juts out into the Atlantic over which you must drive. Make it across and your feet will not touch the ground until you play your second. Fail and its bye, bye ball.

9. Tom Morris: St Andrews, Old. 18th. 356-yard par 4

I challenge any golfer not to fantasise, while striding over the Swilken Bridge, that this is the last hole of the Open and you are in the lead. Wave to the imaginary galleries as you reach the green. A par 4 and you are champion, but spare a thought for Doug Sanders!

Even though there are more than 400 courses in Scotland from which to choose, many visitors arrive in the country under the impression that there are only a handful — the ones they have seen on television during the Open Championship.

The spectre of such visitors, particularly of the American variety rears its ugly head from time to time. Most of us have seen the archetypal ones who fly across the pond to play the Old Course at *Snanders*, complete with two-tone crocodile skin shoes, tartan trousers, caddies and video cameras at the ready to capture their appalling efforts for posterity. Five hours later they have ruined the day for anyone who wants a traditional three-hour, bag-slung-over-the-back bounce game.

Yet their wads of dollars are most welcome and tourist authorities have a welter of statistics which indicate that Scottish golf clubs have resources which are ripe for development, even for visitors from south of the Border.

For example, in England there are twice as many golfers as there are club memberships available. In Europe only ten per cent of those who want to play golf have the opportunity to do so. In America a golf course would have to be opened every day from now until the year 2000 to meet demand.

On the other side of the coin, according to the figures, 70 per cent of Scottish clubs have no waiting list . . . in other words there are plenty of spare tee-off times in Scotland which could be filled by an enormous surplus of golfing tourists.

Thus the picture was painted at a 'Golf in Scotland' seminar arranged by the Scottish Tourist Board in 1989 at the Marine Hotel, North Berwick, and attended by 140 mainly tourism-orientated delegates.

If the potential is obvious, the problems are equally clear. Most visiting golfers — and they are not all as bad as they are sometimes painted — are lured by the five Open Championship venues and are generally unaware that Scotland is a Pandora's box of golf.

These five, especially the Old Course, St Andrews, are unable to meet the demand. Therefore it seems sensible to direct the overspill elsewhere.

It is hard to criticise the clubs. Most exist for the sole benefit of members, with no profit-making motive. The carrot is that subscriptions on the quieter courses have been shown to be capable of reduction of £200 to £90, the difference being made up by visitors' fees. The cost to members is that their course will be busier.

The Scottish Tourist Board is coming to terms with the fact that overseas golfers need educated about the wealth of lesser-known courses, and that literature, including their own, featuring pictures and articles on St Andrews, which least needs the publicity, can be harmful.

The point still remains that a development plan is being put together and an opportunity exists for clubs to increase their income, for example through tours which feature one championship course and several lesser-known and easier to play ones. What price privacy?

Herald Club Golf has learned of a few of these 'hidden gems' on the west coast and islands.

MACHRIE

Travelling to Machrie, on the island of Islay, is easier these days than in the early part of the century when it took a full day's journey including two ferry trips. At the invitation of the Machrie Hotel and charter airline Merlin, I made it in just 18 minutes from Glasgow. That way it was possible to have 18 holes over the splendidly isolated 6,226-yard, par 71 links course, a sumptuous meal in the hotel, and then return home by early evening.

Transport was in a nippy little machine called the *Sorcerer's Apprentice* and continuing the theme there is to be found a hole, the 17th, called *Ifrinn*, the Gaelic word for hell. Partnering hotel proprietor Murdo Macpherson's son Andrew there was another sinister experience in store — losing a pound to former England goal-keeper Gordon Banks, who was there on business and playing along with leading Scots amateur Colin Dalgleish. The debt, naturally, was settled with a Scottish pound note.

The course is completely unspoilt, has many blind spots and attention to the *Strokesaver Guide* is essential. Improvements are taking place also through the work of three greens staff headed by St Andrews-trained David Woodburne. And, as the club approaches its centenary in 1991, there are plans to improve the clubhouse and leisure facilities and expand the accommodation by adding two time-share projects.

When there's the threat of a green burning under the summer sun, they do the obvious thing and call the fire brigade. No one dials 999 because the machine in question is based on the course and is there just for the purpose of hosing water on the greens in time of drought. The ancient vehicle, which could be called 'the Greens Goddess', registration GXE 16, is believed to have been used originally at a former RAF base on the island before finding a home at Machrie. Murdo explained: 'It is an ideal way of watering the greens. The tank holds 500 gallons of water which is pumped from two burns at the course.' They get only about 12 miles to the gallon — but it's still a lot cheaper than a sprinkler system.

There is a bit of history to the place as well with a competition, the Western Isles Open, which has roots stretching back to 1901. The tournament was resurrected in 1985 as an annual event and the format is identical to the one held at the turn of the century and which was won by Englishman J. H. Taylor in an event which the Royal and Ancient have confirmed as having been the first in the world to put up a first prize of £100.

Taylor had a 3 at the final hole to defeat a Scot, James Braid, who nevertheless won £40 as runner-up — £15 more than he received for winning the Open Championship the previous week. Before 1985, when it became the domain of amateurs, it was played only once more — in 1935 when it was won by Jimmy McDowall, then professional at Turnberry.

Who knows what might have become of the tournament had the *Sorcerer's Apprentice* been around then?

KYLES OF BUTE

Scotland is well blessed with some of the greatest jewels in the crown of the world's golf courses. Tripping off the tongue come names like St Andrews, Turnberry, Gleneagles, Muirfield, Troon, Carnoustie, Kyles of Bute . . . Kyles of what?

Well, the Kyles of Bute club may not quite be an Augusta National, but therein lies a golfing spirit as true as you will find anywhere; one of Scotland's dozens of unsung gems. Unlike the armies of greens and clubhouse staff that exist on the more famous courses and clubs, there are none here. Instead it is a do-it-yourself job by a group of committed members who voluntarily keep the nine-hole course at the southern end of the Cowal peninsula in order.

Amid the spartan nature of the place there is an element of Utopia. Views down the Kyles and across to the Island of Bute as you drive into

Tighnabruaich are as spectacular as you will see anywhere in Scotland, Gleneagles included, scenery which exists over most of the short and bunkerless but nevertheless testing 4,778-yard, par-66 course.

A state of temperance may furthermore be suggested by the unlicensed clubhouse yet the hospitality is generous, as anyone who has partaken of it before duffing their tee shot and losing a ball at the deceptively simple 112-yard first will vouch. With the advent of the five-hour round it is also a pleasure to have the course virtually to yourself and complete the double circuit in little more than two hours, your opponent, should he be local, smiling as he beats you.

The good people of Tighnabruaich also have the ability to laugh at themselves in adversity.

Iffrin, as we learned at Machrie, is the Gaelic word for hell. It is also the name of the 6th hole at the club. In this context it might be suitable to rename the course *Purgadair*. It is the Gaelic word for Purgatory, a place the voluntary greens staff might think they are in whilst mowing the fairways on warm, insect-infested evenings.

Lest any of the 196 members worry that this is a gross insult to their course let me quickly, by way of explanation, switch to a corrupt form of Latin. The legend at the foot of the unofficial coat of arms of Tighnabruaich reads *Rainio et Midgeo*, which needs no translation. Above the words are featured on one side a midgie donning Wellington boots, and on the other a bottle of whisky, the entire work topped with a large fish which, apparently, are easier to catch on the Kyles than birdies are on the course.

The club's pride and joy is its vintage Massey Ferguson tractor which is kept in good working order by Neil Galbraith, a forester by occupation but whose mechanical skills have saved the club thousands of pounds.

Members Jim Carruthers, Scott Turner, Tom Nicolson, Ian Wilson, John Whyte, and Alistair Chambers take it in turns to drive the tractor over their designated fairways, while Tom Whyte tends all the greens and puts this knowledge to good use. He is the club champion and holds the course record of 64. The exercise keeps annual subscriptions down to £30 for men and women, and £10 for juniors.

The club was founded in 1907, the course hewn out of wild moorland. But it fell into disuse after the Second World War during which the ground was used for training tank crews. The course lay fallow for around 20 years before the local community made the effort to re-establish it.

Fairways and greens have been improved progressively since, by an ambitious committee. The new clubhouse was opened by Wilbur Muirhead, a former captain of the Royal and Ancient, and in 1987 the course was bought from the Forestry Commission for a modest sum of

Kyles of Bute

less than £20,000. An equivalent figure has just been spent on improving drainage, and the appointment of the club's first green-keeper has been discussed.

The 6th, at 404 yards the longest on the course, is by no means as bad as its name suggests although the tee shot requires a substantial carry over heavy rough. It is the 7th, named MacTavish's after the owner prior to the Forestry Commission, a severely sloping, downhill 258-yarder which invites trouble especially for the fairway mowers.

The Haggs Castle club had an involvement in the resurrection of the course in the 1960s. The late James MacLean, a former member at Haggs, moved from Glasgow to the Kyles area where, missing his golf, he was intrigued to discover the overgrown course. Along with his friend George Symington, he was instrumental in having the ground returned from the commission who had requisitioned it at the beginning of the war. With the help of some of his old friends from Haggs Castle, the course was restored. It could be said of the course that there are fewer places more worthy of lifting your head.

PORT BANNATYNE

Going down to the port in modern golfing parlance, is likely to conjure up pictures of Puerto Banus, Spain's elaborate 19th-hole millionaires' paradise. However, there are other less exotic venues nearer home which can be just as much fun — like the Island of Bute's Port Bannatyne.

The 13-hole course (the first five are played twice) is one venue for the Firth of Clyde Open, which dates back to 1887, and has records from 1898. It is claimed by the organisers, the Associated Clubs of Clyde, to be the oldest surviving club competition in the world.

The original qualification for entry was that players had to come from towns and villages with a pier in the firth. Now 11 clubs take part, the boundary being a line between Gourock and Strone Point. Others are Skelmorlie, Blairmore and Strone, Cowal, Gourock, Rothesay, Millport, Largs Kelburne, Largs Routenburn, Inellan, and Kyles of Bute for the competition, which has a handicap limit of 10.

Some clubs travel by fishing boat, but even without this facility, going down to the port has its attractions. For a Vauxhall Classic team match, it involved a car journey from Helensburgh down the Cowal peninsula and a ferry trip longer than a good drive (as later attempts verified) from Colintraive. If you are lucky, the hosts who meet you on the other side, will take you for an early morning fortified coffee before introducing you to the rigours of the course, which is of indeterminate age but thought to date back to the turn of the century.

Locals will tell you that the reason you seldom get a bad lie on the hilly fairways is because the course was closed for play and used for grazing in the 1960s, the sheep dung from that period giving the grass a rich texture.

At 4,730-yards, par 68 (SSS 63), few holes are more than a drive and a wedge but the subtle slopes mean local knowledge is a key factor. At least that was the excuse for our team, who lost 3-2, yours truly finding the form of vice-captain Andy Williamson too much to cope with.

But compensation was at hand, with his hospitality just as good as his golf. It may not have been champagne as in Puerto Banus, down to the port in this instance involving generous quantities of a local elixir, vodka and Irn Bru, but it took the pain out of defeat.

SHISKINE

What would it cost to have Severiano Ballesteros or Jack Nicklaus design a few new holes on your course? Think of a figure, double it, add a few noughts, an arm and a leg, and you will be just about there.

Information gleaned from a dusty attic at Shiskine Golf Club, in the

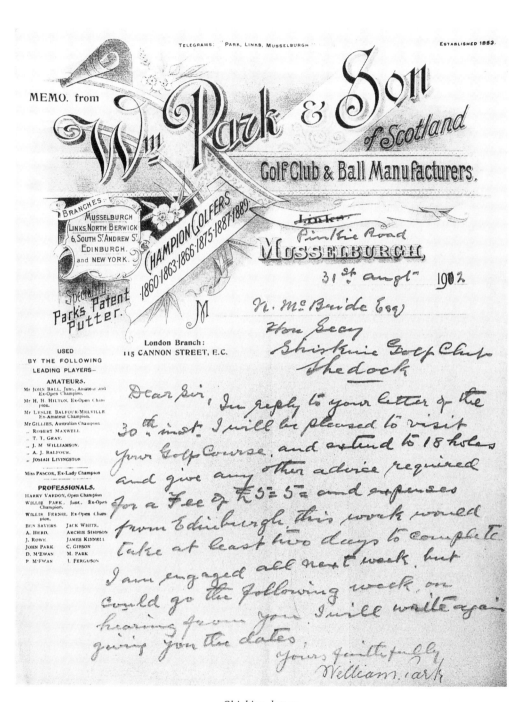

MEMO. from **Wm Park & Son** *of Scotland*

Golf Club & Ball Manufacturers.

TELEGRAMS: PARK, LINKS, MUSSELBURGH   ESTABLISHED 1863.

BRANCHES:
MUSSELBURGH
LINKS, NORTH BERWICK
6, SOUTH St ANDREW S^t
EDINBURGH.
and NEW YORK.

CHAMPION GOLFERS
1860·1863·1866·1875·1887·1889·

Specialty
Park's Patent Putter.

London Branch:
115 CANNON STREET, E.C.

Links
Pinkie Road
MUSSELBURGH,
31st Augt 1902

USED
BY THE FOLLOWING
LEADING PLAYERS—

AMATEURS.
Mr JOHN BALL, Junr., Amateur and Ex-Open Champion,
Mr H. H. HILTON, Ex-Open Champion,
Mr LESLIE BALFOUR-MELVILLE Ex-Amateur Champion,
Mr GILLIES, Australian Champion
„ ROBERT MAXWELL
„ T. T. GRAY.
„ J. M WILLIAMSON.
„ A. J. BALFOUR.
„ JOSIAH LIVINGSTON

Miss PASCOE, Ex-Lady Champion

PROFESSIONALS.
HARRY VARDON, Open Champion
WILLIE PARK, Junr., Ex-Open Champion.
WILLIE FERNIE, Ex-Open Champion.
BEN SAYERS   JACK WHITE.
A. HERD.   ARCHIE SIMPSON
J. ROWE.   JAMES KINNELL
JOHN PARK   C. GIBSON
D. M'EWAN   M. PARK
P M'EWAN   I. FERGUSON

N. Mc Bride Esq)
Hon Secy
Shiskine Golf Club
Shedock

Dear Sir, In reply to your letter of the
30th inst. I will be pleased to visit
your Golf Course, and extend to 18 holes
and give any other advice required
for a Fee of £5=5= and expenses
from Edinburgh this work would
take at least two days to complete
I am engaged all next week, but
could go the following week, on
hearing from you. I will write again
giving you the dates,

Yours faithfully
William Park

Shiskine letter

village of Blackwaterfoot, Arran, reveals that even allowing for inflation, monopoly money has not always been necessary for the services of those with an Open Championship record.

The cost in 1912 for advice from twice Open champion Willie Park Jr of Musselburgh was precisely five guineas, or in present money £5.25 — about enough for a round of drinks and a quick bash on the fruit machine after the Sunday morning four-ball. Expenses were extra.

Yet even in those early days a championship record was clearly a valuable asset, as witness the elaborate letterhead which boasts of six successes, the four others belonging to his father of the same name, including the first in 1860.

It would not, however, be true to say that no expense was spared by Wm Park & Son. There is evidence of shrewd economy. One can deduce that a vast quantity of letterheads were printed in the 1900s and lasted longer than expected. Hence the overwriting of the zero in 1902 with a one.

Shiskine eventually commissioned Park to construct the extra nine holes for an all-inclusive fee of £600, work beginning on 30 September 1912, 'the owner to supply about 30 tons of manure' with a completion date of May the following year. Clearly construction times have increased since then, as has fertiliser technology. The original nine holes were designed by another Open champion, Willie Fernie of Troon, and opened in 1897.

This irresistible historical tittle-tattle is by no means without relevance to today. Shiskine fancies itself as a kind of winter Algarve, albeit a little chillier. The course is open every day, all year round, whatever the weather, and always using the proper greens. Locals will tell you that unless you are really unlucky, the winter weather there is far milder than on the mainland.

The club has launched a winter golf challenge with a difference and which is open to anyone with an official club handicap. The village's main hotel, the Kinloch, is sponsoring a trophy plus other prizes.

The competition, the Arran Challenge, is over 36 holes which — here's the novelty — can be played any time in a ten-day period in December. This to allow for the possibility of bad weather interfering with sailings from Ardrossan to Brodick. A similar tournament for women has been introduced in 1990.

Andrew Donaldson, the club captain, said: 'It will be good for the course and good for those who get weary of life in the cities and towns in the long winter months. The weather is often quite brilliant at that time of year, but we have to remember that occasionally the sea can be quite rough and the ferry can get stuck at Ardrossan. That is why we are calling it the Arran Challenge. If the winner happens to come from the mainland then it will be apparent that he is a tough, determined character.'

Play is over three circuits of the 12-hole course — 12 holes? Did not Willie Park Jr charge £600 in 1912 for extending it to 18?

It seems that he did complete the job, but six holes fell into disuse during the First World War. Yet another Open champion, James Braid, designed six holes to take it up to 18 again in 1937, but the Second World War put paid to that. Now club members believe it is the only 12-hole course in the world — and why not 12? They can be completed comfortably in two hours and, after all, 18 holes is an arbitrary number just because that was how many St Andrews had when the game began to expand.

Mr John Robertson, who is in his 80s and who walked over the course with Braid, said: 'I suppose it was always destined to remain a 12-hole course no matter the ambitions of the various committees at the time.'

MILLPORT

With a host of clubs celebrating their centenaries, nostalgia is at an all-time high. Millport is a case in point. The old first tee on a hill called Mount Pisgah was restored and members donned period dress in an effort to recreate one of the club's oldest photographs, dated 1892.

As can be seen on page 123 the result is impressive but two differences can be spotted. One is the old clubhouse, which is no longer there, whereas the other can be put down to sheer enthusiasm: there are more people on the tee.

Thirteen figures can be seen on the old photo, 48 on the 1988 version. It can be concluded that in the present golfing era there is more danger than there used to be of falling off the tee, a situation recognised by one member who arrived equipped with mountaineering gear, including a rope.

In total, six holes of the original course were resurrected by greenkeeping staff on the basis of plans and pictures in a fascinating and impeccably researched history of the club, *Beyond Mount Pisgah*, written by Dugald McIntyre.

From this book it can be gleaned that 100 years and more ago readers of the *Glasgow Herald* had a keen interest in golf (some things don't change). Indeed, it is said that the meeting at which the Millport club was formed was inspired by an article in the *Herald* which suggested that the prosperity of Cumbrae could be increased by building a golf links.

The vision of island prosperity may not have come to pass, but the golf club certainly did, aided by a welter of mainland members, notably from the Glasgow Club. Even today around 60 per cent of members live away from the island.

McIntyre's history reveals far more than parochial interests. George Duncan, long before he won the Open Championship at Deal in 1920, had made his mark at Millport, firstly by beating then Open champion James Braid in a challenge match in 1911 with a 73 to a 76 and then in 1913 beating J. H. Taylor, Ted Ray and Braid with a celebrated round of 67.

Despite the presence of a large crowd of Glasgow Fair holiday-makers, the only untoward incident involved a lady who got in the way of a Braid shot and diverted the ball back into play with her hat.

Back on the tee at Mount Pisgah 1988-style, the six resurrected holes were proving to be a test of stamina as well as golf. They were virtually tee to green with no fairway. Competitors were each issued with six balls of the tattie variety. Few returned with that number, having bashed them about with hickory cleeks and mashies which had long been gathering dust in attics and cellars.

The first ball was driven by captain Jim Steven, who, with his wife May, also had the distinction of being acclaimed the most authentically dressed.

The competition was won by juniors Robert Glenroy and Caroline Lennox with sub-par net scores — a tribute to their golfing prowess and mountain-goat agility.

STORNOWAY

Bringing in the golfing New Year on a Hebridean parkland course might seem like going out of bounds with an opening tee shot, which I must admit I did. The 5,119-yard, par-68 course at Stornoway is certainly outward bound, but there are clues which suggest this western outpost has a pedigree which can match many of its more renowned mainland counterparts.

Partaking of refreshment in the ultra-friendly clubhouse to celebrate not just the start of 1990 but the beginning of the club's centenary year, the eye is caught by photographs hanging on the wall of old Tom Morris and Horace Hutchinson, respectively the best professional and amateur golfer of 100 years ago.

As the minutes of the first 43 years are missing, speculation is rife about a prestigious start.

Certainly, it is known that old Tom designed the nine-hole course at Askernish in South Uist in 1890, so it is not unreasonable to think he may have come a little further north while he was in the area. Perhaps Hutchinson joined him on this island-hopping safari, but we will not know for sure unless these minutes come to light — which in a sense would be a pity as a little mystique can go a long way.

Stornoway is not exactly the place to go for a day's outing — much

Millport before

Millport after

better to spend a week. The course is accessed by either a four-hour ferry trip from Ullapool or an hour's flight from Glasgow. The latter method, as well as being more comfortable, is also more appropriate because the airport is constructed on the site of the original links at Steinish, planes touching down where old Tom may well have trod.

Nowadays, the course is located nearer town on the former Lady Lever Park, and was constructed from money raised by a successful Land Court claim against the Air Ministry for loss of the course during the Second World War. The war memorial, on a hill above the course, is there as a reminder of how it came to be.

Visitors are invariably surprised at the quality of the course, and a small part of the reason is accidental.

One of the gems unearthed in the club's lively 60-page centenary magazine is that the lush greens came about because of a former green-keeper's error in administering ten times the specified amount of ammonia and iron aimed at eliminating daisies. Timely heavy rain saved the day and the outcome, as the greens convener of the time, Dan Reid, recalls, 'was the most verdant greens imaginable with every daisy perishing'.

There is also a hole, Dardanelles, a 547-yard double dog-leg which has been described in a leading golf magazine as 'the most difficult par five in Europe'.

Another hazard is that most of the 190 male members seem to have two names, one by which they introduce themselves, and another by which they are commonly known. Thus the two (victorious) opponents of captain Chris Kelso and myself: Iain and Malcolm, are called, bizarrely, Gordy and Hoggles by everyone else.

Seventy juniors swell the ranks, but curiously there are only eight women members. This is not, as it might seem, the result of Hebridean male chauvinism but, as Chris suggests, caused by the absence of a club professional. 'I am sure more women would take up the game if lessons were available and we are hoping in a year or two to appoint a professional-cum-clubmaster,' he said.

Centenary events were to include a competition having its start on two holes reconstructed by the airport on the original course.

Fasten seat belts for take off.

This article brought a curious reaction from the golf columnist of the *tornoway Gazette:*

> The *Glasgow Herald* had an interesting adulatory article on the club and its centenary. It is high in praise of the course, the atmosphere in the clubhouse, and the centenary magazine. Mind you, some of us thought that Chris was taking a chance allowing any visitor, let alone a journalist, go round with Hoggles.

Whether the columnist was aware that Hoggles is, in fact, my brother-in-law remains to be found out.

HYSKEIR

DENNIS SHERRIFS

Gifford in East Lothian may hold the distinction of having the lowest subscription fees in the country; The Honourable Company of Edinburgh Golfers is still probably regarded as being the most exclusive. But step forward the men from Hyskeir as having the weirdest set-up.

There are six of them, three with little interest in playing, but who do their bit to look after the course. They have no subscription fees to fork out, but to get to their 'course' they must be taken by helicopter . . . and air-lifted back!

They are the men who man the Hyskeir lighthouse, a rock station stuck in the Atlantic, six miles south of the island of Canna and ten miles south-west of Rhum in the Outer Hebrides.

A lot of hard work, which began in 1982, saw them design and create their own golf course — all six holes, complete with bunkers and the perpetual water hazard — the Atlantic. Bill Gault, John Kermode, and Neil Brown are the three 'golf nuts' who spent their spare time honing their short game.

Explained Aberdonian Gault, who in his youth was a single-figure handicapper: 'It's really more of a pitch-and-putt circuit, but it serves its purposes. We would like to extend it, but for obvious reasons this is impossible. The rock measures approximately half a mile long, and quarter of a mile wide.

'It certainly is a far cry from the surroundings of the lighthouse station which sits on the championship Turnberry course, but we probably derive as much pleasure and satisfaction as our colleagues who play over that famous course. And I would imagine that we get more opportunity to sharpen our short game.'

Not surprisingly, the weather conditions can be a bit of a problem, to say the least. And there is another major hazard, added Bill, who, like his colleagues, spends four weeks on duty and then returns to the mainland for the next four weeks.

'Every now and then one of us will open up our shoulders, with the result that there is a high percentage of lost balls.'

Certainly a case of: 'For those in peril on the tee.'

OLD COURSE, ST ANDREWS (BACKWARDS)

The Old Course, St Andrews, is not exactly a hidden gem, but it could be described as such the way it was played early in 1989 — backwards. That was how the world's most hallowed links was always negotiated until the mid-to-late 19th century. *Herald* Club Golf took a trip back in time to find out what it was like.

It is a rare opportunity for your average golfer to follow not in the footsteps of Arnold Palmer, Jack Nicklaus and Seve Ballesteros as can be done at most times of the year, but of Tom Morris Jr and Allan Robertson, pioneers of the professional era.

They took what is called the left-hand route, the sinistral way to fame. Why the switch was made to the right-hand version, the one recognised today as the ultimate Open Championship course, is unclear. But the St Andrews Link Trust, custodians of the course, had, at the request of the Royal and Ancient Club, taken the step back in time for both sentimental and practical reasons, the latter being to give parts of the course a rest.

Fewer than 100 visitors took the opportunity, but there was one notable happening during the R and A winter medal.

It was won by retired timber merchants Bob Cumming and Eric Donaldson, who last partnered each other no fewer than 54 years ago when they played against England in a boys' international at Birkdale.

Only once has this course been used for a championship, and that was by mistake. It had been overlooked that the week of the left-hand course coincided with the Amateur in 1886. Competitors began playing that way, and so it continued until Harold Hutchinson triumphed.

At the best of times a caddie is required to help unravel the mysteries of the Old Course, and doubly so playing backwards, when the course is reduced by 77 yards from the usual 6,566 but retaining the par of 72. The feeling of disorientation on the first tee is immense as you point yourself not to the first green but the 17th.

'The line is the Swilken Bridge,' said my caddie, Bill Gunn, who then watched in horror an awful hook, the ball landing between two parked cars on The Links road and taking a big bounce towards a house.

'Did it break a window?' I asked anxiously.

'I'm no worried about that. I only hope it came back on to the course,' came the reply.

Now here's a man on the side of a would-be golfer, even if the ball was retrieved ignominiously from a domestic basement.

This was the Tom Morris hole the other way round. Obviously, it must be called Sirrom Mot, which somehow does not have the same ring to it. Neither does the green, probably the most famous in the world, look quite right, long and thin instead of short and fat when you approach it down the normal 17th fairway, where the notorious Road Hole bunker looms large. From there, the great links are turned into a slicer's dream.

More than 100 years ago there was said to have been a great debate about whether to favour the right or left course, the seven huge double greens allowing this peculiar choice, but from a brief taste the correct decision appears to have been made, even if it was a lot of fun.

One aspect of the game there is consistent, however, and that is the pungent humour of the caddies. 'Aye, you don't believe in short-cuts,' was the response to one wayward tee shot. Another withering conversation went like this:

'Have I found a bunker?'

'I would say that.'

'It did bounce though.'

'Aye, but only the once.'

The history books tell us that this kind of endearing patter, a view of life almost from a pedestal above all others, has been going on for centuries. It is recorded that one caddie, after having watched the enthusiastic efforts of former Prime Minister A. J. Balfour, said: 'Wi' his height and my brains, we'd mak a grand foursome.'

Another caddie, having been to a poetry evening the night before, made ingenious use of a line from 'Charge of the Light Brigade' which went: 'Their's not to reason why, Their's but to do or die. Into the Valley of Death, Rode the Six Hundred.'

At the 16th, he gave his man a club and told him to hit the ball 'ower that hump'. His man protested that this was at least four yards off line and must have squirmed at the retort.

'Your's not to reason why,' he recalled from the poem, then ad-libbed aggressively: 'Your's but tae dae whit you're bloody well telt!'

I tried tae dae whit I was telt and shot a humbling 91, 20 more than the record set by Willie Auchterlonie in 1897. Pity it wasn't five shots worse. I could have claimed it as a backwards 69.

GLASGOW GAILES

An invitation from that fine body of men, the Glasgow Golf Club, to play their second course at Gailes, seemed too good to turn down, even in February. The club were anxious to dispel their image as a closed shop, and have been laying out a welcome mat for visiting parties. A pleasant experience is in store for those who take up the offer, especially if you make time for a spot of lunch beforehand.

I was recommended, and can do so myself in turn, the mince, topped by a poached egg with as many tatties and neeps as you can manage, and washed down by a bottle of bicentenary wine.

On the course, rubber shoes are rarely required, even in winter. The course is usually as dry as a bone and lush enough to make the preferred lie rule well nigh redundant. The bunkers are almost a pleasure to be in. Women, contrary to some opinions, are also welcome, although they should be aware that they will have to play off the same tees as the men.

The course is generally flat but with subtle undulations particularly on the greens, where the advice is to take a little less borrow than you think. Aficionados liken the course to St Andrews in that appreciation comes gradually rather than immediately. They use expressions like 'jewel' and 'sleeping giant' and it is hard to argue when you are enjoying yourself on a full stomach.

It was also a rare case of yours truly actually winning a match. Personally, I credit the poached egg, though the local knowledge of my partner, Gailes convener Alistair McLay, may also have had something to do with it.

IN SEARCH OF A CHAMPION

Where is the man to match Willie Auchterlonie, the last home-based Scot to win the Open championship? And why has no one done this since his triumph way back in 1893? The weather is certainly a factor in that there is little more than six months prime playing time in a season, but to leave it at that would be to gloss over more deep-rooted reasons why, in the last century, Scotland's domination of the game has switched to England, then America, and now back to Europe.

The truth of the matter is that Scotland's 400-plus clubs, collectively a revered institution, are geared to catering for moderately competent players with few real aspirations, and not to producing champions. Although there are exceptions, juniors are generally treated as pests, practice facilities are woefully inadequate, and coaching is minimal, even if it is, by some accounts, better than it used to be. Three universities — Stirling, St Andrews and Dundee — are now offering golf scholarships but this is little more than a step in the right direction when you compare it with the intensely competitive American collegiate set-up.

The treatment of juniors was a question raised by Alex Law when he was junior convener at the Barrhead club of Fereneze, after his juniors had won the Fleming Watson Trophy, a competition among member clubs of the Brand Putter League.

These youngsters and their like, he will tell you, are the ones who will be charged with responsibility for the game in Scotland a generation hence. Alex, who describes himself as a progressive radical, is on their side, so when he takes a dirty great swipe at general club attitudes towards juniors, including his beloved Fereneze, it is perhaps worth listening to.

He is extremely concerned at the likelihood that a vast array of talent at Scottish clubs is disappearing down the plug-hole at an alarming rate simply because the powers that be at club level are at best only passively interested and at worst downright antagonistic.

Each of the nine juniors who played for Fereneze in their victorious season provided, as is the norm, their own balls, shoes, and equipment. Access to their home course is restricted — again, not unusual.

In other words, what right have the club membership to bask in any glory brought to them by their budding talent? The club did provide club jerseys, thereby instilling a sense of team spirit and loyalty, but it has to be asked whether this kind of gesture is enough.

'If Scotland is to produce outstanding golfers, potential Open champions, then golf clubs, and I include my own, must overcome what I would call conservative traditions, which are a cancer in our game,' said Alex. 'The worst types are the super-reactionaries at clubs like Prestwick and Muirfield,' he continued, mischievously adding a dig at these revered establishments: 'These places would be better used for housing developments!'

These 'traditions' are rules such as that young players, no matter how good, must play off forward junior tees, play only at certain times — and even then always give way to seniors — be segregated in clubhouses, and generally be regarded as nuisances.

Unlike many clubs, however, Fereneze allow juniors to compete in their club championship. Campbell Elliot, now assistant to Niall Cameron at Royal St George's, Sandwich, was, in 1987, the first junior to be club champion.

Alex, a former club captain, added: 'The very best juniors are always likely to be hand-picked by county unions and coached under their wings. We could do with far more of this. I would like to see a broadening of the base — clubs extending formal coaching to, say, 15-handicappers and trying to get them down to single figures quickly, and allowing them to play off medal tees in supervised competition. Many are far more qualified to do so than the majority of seniors.

'Coaching could be sponsored by local companies, perhaps owned by members, so that the club professional, often quite unjustly expected to carry out this function for nothing, does not bear the full brunt. Balls and equipment for team members could also be provided by this means.

'It concerns me that juniors who go on to take further education are often completely lost to the game because they cannot afford to keep it up. Perhaps clubs should ask themselves if there is any way of lessening the burden, even by providing heavily subsidised subscriptions, so that their interest is retained.

'I would also challenge schools to take golf on board and get in with their local professional. Swimming always seems to be an important sport on physical education curricula, so why not golf?'

The Fleming Watson competition is well-established, begun by Andrew Fleming, a member at Cathkin Braes and former president of the Brand Putter League, and Bill Watson, professional at Whitecraigs. The need to encourage juniors has long been recognised. The question is whether enough is being done.

Fereneze later spent £250 on coaching, with the Golf Foundation adding a further £80. Coaching was to be undertaken by club professional Andy Armstrong with special attention to those with handicaps higher than 20.

The treatment of juniors is a question also posed by John Mulgrew, professional at the Normandy Driving Range in Renfrew. John is far from the archetypal dreamer. He is a businessman first and a golf professional second, with his feet well and truly on the ground. But he has an ultimate ideal.

It is a national golf centre which, being realistic, is unlikely to come about until the next millennium, if at all. But there is no reason why the theory should not be teed up now and given a good thrash down the fairway.

This centre, open to the public, would include a testing 18-hole course, a par 3 course, driving range, residential accommodation, and extensive practice areas for practising a wide variety of shots. There would also be a fun area for juniors which is significant in the masterplan.

He says: 'My pet hate is that juniors tend to be overlooked and even frowned upon by many golf members when they are, and should be regarded as, the lifeblood of the game. Yet when you look at many golf clubs the juniors are simply ignored.'

Mulgrew is one of only a few golf professionals who have a set-up even remotely approaching this. He shares his time between the Normandy Driving Range and the Renfrew club, just a wedge distance away, and is thus able to combine teaching on course with the more theoretical approach on the range.

Fifteen years ago driving ranges were virtually unknown in Scotland. Now there are ranges also at Hamilton, Motherwell, Uddingston, Bishopbriggs, Stevenston, Prestwick, Ingliston, Cumbernauld and Inverclyde. The last named is the nearest thing to a national golf centre.

The range at Inverclyde has more than a dozen bays, there are six golf holes, and an area with greens and bunkers for practice. It is used frequently by the Scottish Golf Union for boys' coaching, but the centre is shared with many other sports, including tennis, sailing, gymnastics and squash.

Coaching is certainly catered for by the Scottish Golf Union among those identified as potential international material, but to get to that stage a young player's future can be in the laps of the gods. It depends very much on whether a club is either willing or able to respond.

A rapidly growing number of boys' summer competitions have produced an impressive, if rather haphazard circuit which, over the eight-week summer holiday period, can place as much pressure on a teenager as there is on a professional on the European Tour. Sadly, unlike the seniors, there is no order of merit for boys' events, the competitions being run by so wide a variety of organisations that such an arrangement would be problematic. There was an awards scheme, sponsored by the Royal Bank of Scotland, which fell by the wayside in 1983, and many players and officials feel that such a system is worth resurrecting.

Practice facilities are also lacking, a point raised by former Walker Cup player and captain, Charlie Green, still a top player at the age of 57, who believes the odds are stacked against today's generation of young golfers who, nevertheless, are pioneering a new approach to the game.

'When I started playing it seemed I was the only one on the practice ground but the whole scene is changing. You can see it at Dumbarton and Cardross where I am a member. The practice grounds are busy. In my time there was a tendency to improve by playing round after round, but you have to combine both,' said the three-times Scottish Amateur champion and two-time holder of the Scottish stroke-play title.

'I think there is more coaching, too. If a club has a professional he is coaching all the juniors which is getting them off to a better start. Things are improving, but there are still too many golfers who learn by themselves and faults are well developed by the time they seek lessons, unlike in America where the first thing a father does is ensure a child is coached before he plays.'

Does this all mean that Scotland is likely to produce a world-beater?

Green said that Open champions nowadays are international players. Tony Jacklin, Sandy Lyle, and Nick Faldo falling into this category. The last comparatively untravelled Britons to win were Max Faulkner in 1951 and Fred Daly in 1947. 'When you look at the record after that you have winners like Bob Charles, Ken Nagle, Ben Hogan, and Bobby Locke — every one a world-wide player, and I think it is going to stay that way,' he added.

He identified the most prominent Scots of the last 35 years as John Panton, the late Eric Brown, and globetrotters Bernard Gallacher and Sam Torrance, none of whom have won a major. At the top end of the scale the European Tour has become a success story, but all prominent players have to start somewhere.

He continued: 'This is where we are up against it in Scotland. Practice facilities are dreadful even if they are improving slightly. I reckon I have played around 200 courses in Scotland and from what I have seen only about one in 20 has a good practice area. Usually it is either a wee strip of ground well away from the clubhouse or, like Cardross, a sloping area. The ideal practice ground is a flat area about 250 yards long by 80 yards wide.

'Neither have I seen any facilities in Scotland for practising in wet weather like there are in many clubs abroad, where you can play under cover.'

He reasoned that designers who built courses 80 and more years ago had to cram 18 holes into a small area of ground often set aside for golf because it was no use for anything else. Under those circumstances the best parts were used for golf holes and the leftovers put aside for practice.

Our climate is another factor against us. A theory sometimes put forward is that this helps Scots because Open Championships are played on windy links courses, conditions which they are used to. Not so, according to Green.

'There are too many days when there is a high wind which does not help to develop a repeating swing. It is easy to develop faults playing regularly in the wind. It is much more preferable to develop a swing in calm conditions, and practice low shots for a windy day rather than the other way round. Then there is the length of the playing season. We are lucky if we get from May to October,' he said.

So the message is that when you say to yourself on the 18th green 'this one for the Open' you are indulging in what is always likely to be a pure fantasy. Heading overseas may be a necessary step on the road to major success, but we can still give our youngsters a better start.

A DEGREE OF HELP

The golf scholarship trail is now a well-trodden path. More than ten years have elapsed since the first Scots went to America, a period during which three Scottish universities, Stirling, St Andrews and Dundee, have responded to the trend with schemes which can confidently be described as soundly based. The American version, however, can still be a lottery.

Taking the trans-Atlantic route with its lure of year-round golf and the glamour of visiting a foreign country can be a dream come true if everything works out, a nightmare if it does not. The chances of finding a college with a tailor-made balance in golf and study are improving but currently the safest advice for the present crop of talented young golfers is to shop around at home first, and elsewhere in Britain, Bath and Swansea offer golf scholarships.

Golf may be more intensive in America where the education system is far more athletically orientated than in Scotland, but here academic standards are generally higher and in addition to specialist golf training the student will, provided all exams are passed, end up with a respected degree unlike the American variety which is not recognised by our Government's department of education and science.

The pioneers in Scotland are Stirling University where eight students are in various stages of a golf scholarship, and there could be more. Dr Ian Thomson, director of physical recreation, has found there is a shortage of applicants fulfilling both the university's entrance requirements (four Highers at B level) and the level of golfing ability (handicap 2 or better).

The only academic concession made is that a degree can be taken over five instead of the usual four years. Sports bursaries for golf worth £1,150 to finance competition expenses and training, and £900 to assist the maintenance grant in that extra year, are provided by three sources. The Royal and Ancient Golf Club donated three to begin with, building up to five a year by 1991, the St Andrews-based Macleod Foundation give four, covering squash and tennis as well as golf, and six come from the university itself.

Dr Thomson said: 'Six outstanding young Scottish golfers who applied to us did not get a place, but did in an American university. It seems that the combination of handicap and Highers is proving too much. My advice is that young golfers should concentrate more on their Highers even if it means not picking up a golf club for six months. It is more important to get into university even without a scholarship.'

Four of the Stirling bursars, including Colin Dalgleish who was the first, had all been to America before becoming disenchanted with the level of emphasis on the academic side and returning home.

Stirling, however, are heavily into sporting achievements. Having won the Scottish Universities championship in 1989 at Montrose for the fifth year in a row, and the British Universities title for three out of five, they have recognised that, unlike in America, competition must be sought outside the education network.

Catriona Lambert, a member at North Berwick and Gullane, and Irish student Vari McGreey went to Spain later in the year to compete in the Spanish Ladies Amateur, and several of the students took part in the World Students Championships the year before in Italy.

One place where there is certainly no lack of opportunity for practice is at St Andrews where the R and A are donating two bursaries a year in a programme which started in 1989, the first two being to Craig Barton of Kilmarnock Barassie, a 5-handicapper when he was accepted, and James Ritchie from Colchester, a 4-handicapper.

Unlike Stirling, there is no concession whatsoever to academic work at St Andrews where the handicap limit for applicants is ten. There were more than ten applicants for the first year and although a low handicap is desirable, potential bursars are well screened to ensure students capable of combining study and golf are taken on.

Dr Martin Farrally, director of physical education, said: 'Academic standards come first but the bursars must show improvement in their standard of golf. Stirling are looking to produce outstanding golfers whereas we take on good golfers and try to make them better. One thing I would like to point out is that bursaries are open to both male and female students.'

Coaching is undertaken by Jim Farmer, former Scottish junior coach, who also helps bursars, who receive £1,000 to cover equipment and competition expenses, map out their summer competitive golf programme.

At Dundee, eight golf bursaries are on offer from 1990, organised and financed by the R and A. Like St Andrews, no concession will be made to academic work. Bursaries are worth £1,000 a year and applicants must have a single-figure handicap.

While it is hoped that other Scottish universities follow suit, places are obviously more limited than in America where there are around 4,000 universities and colleges. Trying to find the right one can be a minefield. One newly introduced service is the Sports Scholarship Foundation, an American agency based at North London College, which flies to Britain some 30 American coaches each year, up to seven of them golf ones, for two-day trials.

They have already placed one Scot, Neil Dunn, at the University of Miami. The foundation is non-profit making but charges £75 for registration and a further £125 if applicants are selected for the trials from which last year there was a success rate in golf of 51 per cent.

Ron Walker, director and co-founder, said: 'We have a look at academic and golfing ability, and our advice is that it will be very difficult to place anyone with a handicap of higher than 4. Academic requirements vary. For a grade one college in the National Collegiate Athletic Association, five O levels and sometimes one or two Highers are required. For others the requirement is less.'

A rather complicated system includes grades two and three in the NCAA, followed by the National Athletic Inter-Collegiate Junior College Athletic Association, and then community and state schools, all offering golf scholarships. The foundation strives to match the student to the best possible and most appropriate college for the individual.

Advice from the Scottish Golf Union, however, is that a visit should be made to the college before making any commitment, even if it means twisting the arm of a favourite uncle for the money. It is also possible to arrange to play in a junior golf tournament giving the opportunity to speak to golf coaches on the spot. Speaking to players who have been through the system is also worthwhile.

Colin Dalgleish, who won the Scottish Amateur title in his first year at Stirling after having attended Ohio State University which produced the likes of Jack Nicklaus, Tom Weiskopf, and Joey Sindelar, said: 'I would estimate that I was able to spend only around half the time playing golf at Stirling than was the case in America. Having said that I think Stirling are doing a good job in combining the two. Previously a good player would have been forced to choose between going to university and letting the golf slip or going full-time without academic backing.'

Dalgleish, who graduated in accountancy at Stirling and is now running a golf travel business from Helensburgh in conjunction with

Derek Crawford

brother Gordon, who operates from Atlanta, added: 'The American system is far more advanced and better geared to turning out athletes who, unlike here, do not have to go outside the college network in an effort to become the best at their chosen sport. To be best in Scotland a golfer will have to go out and compete in open amateur events.

'There is also a far bigger pool of players in America, where perhaps four times as many people go on to take further education than is the case in Scotland. It would be fair to say that academic standards are not as high as they are here but it isn't the case that you can get away with failing everything in America. Strict rules on academic standards are laid down by the National Collegiate Athletic Association.'

This is a view shared by Duncan Weir, a graduate from William and Mary's College in Williamsburg, Virginia, who is now assistant championship secretary at the R and A and who is regularly advising prospective golf scholars on what to expect.

Duncan, who had six Highers and therefore a clear choice between Scotland and America, said: 'That scholarship came about when I was invited to compete in American tournaments after I won the Scottish Boys' title in 1979. In America I met some of the golf coaches who gave me much useful help and advice. Had I not gone to play there it would have made it more difficult to make the right choice.

'But it does depend on where you go. Whereas the choice in Scotland is limited there are thousands of colleges in America which have a golf programme. As a general rule of thumb the stronger ones academically are in the north.'

The variables, he said, are immense. A college might have a good golf coach or a coach who knows nothing about the game and is expert in baseball instead; there might be eight students in golf or 800; there might be easy access to a golf course or it might be miles away; it might be easy to get into a golf team or it might be impossible; a degree course might be good or it might be weak.

'For a lot of people it doesn't work out, but I was lucky and am glad I went. I would certainly do it again, but those intending to go should speak to people who have been and if possible make a visit to America. It might be expensive, but it is well worth it.'

Two golfers the American programme has worked out for recently are Derek Crawford of Sandyhills and Jill Kinloch of Cardross. Derek is now, in 1990, completing his last stretch of a five-year American sojourn with the aim of returning to chase an international team place.

The 24-year-old member of the Sandyhills club in Glasgow and a former youth cap has already been recognised as one of the top 30 out of more than a thousand American college players. The only other Scot to have achieved this distinction, in the form of selection to an honorary all-American team invited to an annual banquet, is the now European Tour player Colin Montgomerie from Troon.

'I have never looked back since I went to America. My game has improved in leaps and bounds and I will get a degree at the end of it,' said the plus-1-handicapper, who had six top ten finishes in the fiercely competitive collegiate 54-hole tournaments in 1989, twice finishing with sub-par aggregates, and regards the banquet in Oklahoma as the highlight.

For more than a year Derek was No. 1 in the University of New Mexico golf team, which itself is ranked No. 15 out of more than 300 college teams.

Jill, in 1989, took part in the prestigious 72-hole National Collegiate Championships at the tough par-73 Palo Alto course in California. A third-year sports management student at the University of Georgia, Jill was a member of the five-strong team which came sixth out of 17, and individually finished 59th out of 102 with rounds of 76, 84, 78 and 79 — her second round being mainly responsible for pushing her down the field — 24 behind the winner, Pat Hurst. She was second best out of several British players, England's Alison Shapcott finishing ahead of her.

Professionals are also finding a degree of help. Blackboard and chalk have rarely been associated with the learning process of the Lords of the Links. Golf professionals, it is often thought, attend instead the School of Hard Knocks, as they have done since the pre-Open championship days of Allan Robertson at St Andrews.

It might come as a surprise, then, to find out that study and examinations are now all the rage. Although Einstein's Theory of Relativity does not quite come into it, lectures and practicals do. Club professionals now must seek qualification, and spend a week each year of their minimum three-year training period at college.

Classes are taken by Scotland's foremost club professionals, such as Brian Anderson (Dalmahoy) — a driving force behind establishing the system in Scotland — Ian Marchbank (Gleneagles Hotel), Bob Jamieson (Turnberry Hotel), and Billy Lockie (Kilmarnock Barassie). They are among the modern trail-blazers and a visit to their shops will provide a glimpse of the standard being set.

Raising this standard, and keeping ahead of developments are the objectives, based on recognition that golf is not only a game. It is a multi-billion pound worldwide going concern as well.

Anyone who thinks that all a young assistant has to do is to tend the shop and mess about on the course would be astonished at what is involved. He or she must learn business, sales, teaching, public relations, crafts, and legislation . . . and that is before there is a chance to go out to practise the easy things like No. 1 iron shots under the wind, with a touch of fade, to a green 220 yards distant.

Training was started on a voluntary basis in 1961, became compulsory in 1970, and residential courses have been on the go since 1984. They are run on a shoestring budget. Students pay for food and accommodation, and the Royal and Ancient Club makes an annual donation.

There are around 750 students (35 women) in various stages of training, almost 100 of whom are in Scotland, and the number has been falling for several years. Malcolm Hulley, head of training at The Belfry-based Professional Golfers' Association, said: 'This is by design. In previous years, the number had been increasing by about five per cent per year. Our mathematics suggested that, at this rate, in 20 years' time, we would effectively double our membership roll. I do not think it is likely that the number of job opportunities will rise accordingly.' The current drain of talent to Europe is causing some concern, but this trend is not thought to be long-lasting, particularly as the PGA is helping other countries set up their own schools.

To reduce numbers, a six-month probationary period was introduced. Although the success of this venture has not been assessed fully, the indications are that it is working. The facility allows for working in a professional's shop without losing amateur status. That way, it is possible for youngsters to change their mind about a career in golf without any lasting damage, in contrast to the separate PGA European Tour qualifying school, entry to which means immediate forfeiture of amateur standing.

This introductory period eliminates some. The handicap limit was dropped from 6 to 4 and entrance examinations were set by the PGA for those without O-level English and Arithmetic. Also, club premises were inspected and only those which came up to standard were approved for taking on an assistant.

'Current club professionals did not go through training like this — so we hope eventually to see higher standards, because the game is becoming more demanding year by year from members and equipment manufacturers. We are trying to stay ahead of developments or, at worst, respond as quickly as we can to change,' added Hulley. 'In the more than ten years I have been with the PGA, shops have improved dramatically, which they have had to because of competition from mail order firms and specialist golf shops. Club professionals are moving into management. The whole world of golf is demanding more from golf.'

Tournament golf is the carrot for many youngsters, but this does not come into the teaching programme, which concentrates solely on learning the game as a trade.

One effect has been to crystallise the decision between tournament or club golf. 'Youngsters tend nowadays to make a more definite choice and identify their limitations earlier. Most who come into the club side do so with the intention of becoming a club professional — but should they improve they might decide to give it a whirl.'

Over the past few years, 40-50 per cent of trainees failed exams at their first attempt, after which the vast majority go on to pass. Hully

Andrew Cullen

expected and, therefore, they are being pushed to a higher level than before.'

Exams are on five subjects — general swing and teaching, repairs, commercial studies, rules of golf, and tournament administration and log book. They must pass all five before they qualify, and are allowed a fourth year and one further re-examination if required.

The log book is particularly revealing. Students must detail their knowledge on more than 50 topics, including shop manner (have you noticed how they are all so polite until you get to know them?), stock control, VAT, computers — even, horror of horrors, appreciating club committee meetings.

Maybe Einstein's Theory of Relativity is a soft option after all.

Such is the attraction of this training that the first university graduate enrolled in 1989. Just over a year previously, Andrew Cullen had been a geography student at Glasgow University contemplating a career in areas like forestry and conservation. The step he took in becoming a trainee assistant at the Royal Burgess Golfing Society of Edinburgh is most unusual for a young man in possession of a BSc degree from a highly respected seat of learning.

'I wanted an outdoor job, but there are few for geography graduates. It was my enjoyment of the game that made up my mind — I like meeting and getting on with people. In my final year I had a chat with George Yuille, the Royal Burgess professional, and I started work there a week after my finals.

'I thoroughly enjoyed my time at university and certainly would do it again. It is good to have a degree as something to fall back on if things do not work out. The only thing I would change is that I would have worked more at my golf. I did not play much during term time, nor did I play for the university team because of academic work on Wednesday afternoons when the matches took place.'

Andrew, whose handicap had been 6 since the age of 14, is more than making up for time lost, and has started out on what is fast becoming the routine way into professional golf — a probationary period during which amateur status is retained so that there is always the choice of opting out without doing any permanent damage.

'If I improve sufficiently, I would like to try in a few years' time for my European Tour card, but if I am to become a club professional, I think I might try for a job abroad.'

To that end, Andrew is studying French and German so that he can teach Europeans in their own language. And with his qualification in geography, he should be able to find his way there no bother at all. Who still thinks that all a golf professional needs to be able to do is to hit a ball?

WHO IS THE
GODFATHER?

An underground organisation known as the golfing mafia is said to exist within the walls of the *Glasgow Heralf* editorial floor. I can neither confirm nor deny this. Suffice to say that there is an editorial spring and autumn outing, a knot of enthusiasts calling themselves the April Shower, who go on tour that month, a Sports Editor's knockout competition and countless ongoing challenge matches. Within the building under the aegis of the *Glasgow Herald* Golf Club, which has non course-owning status with the Scottish Golf Union and which is celebrating its centenary in 1990, there is a Spring and Autumn Meeting, and three knockout competitions.

With such resources at our disposal it is hardly surprising that a wide variety of views on the game have come to light in the Club Golf page. Accordingly there follows a series of invited articles from Doug Gillon (Hilton Park), Elspeth Burnside (Newbattle), Andy MacKay (Paisley), Doug Campbell (Kirkintilloch), John Duncan and Billy Piper (both Stirling), Bill Sutherland (unattached), David Steele (Prestwick St Nicholas), David Bryden (Elderslie) and Tom Shields (unattached), the latter article by courtesy of *Bogeys — The Really Serious Golf Comic*. An article by Eric Wishart (Williamwood) appears at the end of the chapter on Women's Golf. Which one is the Godfather? We all have our own idea.

A GUT FEELING

DOUG GILLON
One's earliest golfing memory can be retraced to a visit to grand-father's house in Leith, a No. 9 iron shot from The Links which was the original home of The Honourable Company of Edinburgh Golfers and whose home is now Muirfield.

At the foot of the stairs stood an antique coat stand, a graveyard for old umbrellas and walking sticks. An inquisitive seven-year-old unearthed two hickory sticks with metal heads.

One, I recall, bore the word 'jigger' while the other, I was told, was something called a putter. 'It's for hitting little balls straight into a hole in the ground.' Sure enough, the flip-top drawer surrendered a couple of peculiar white balls.

To the certain joy of the elders, a few moments' blessed relief was gained as a mischievous child was despatched to the garden, there to essay a swing which has never markedly improved or slowed perceptibly throughout a lifelong love-hate affair.

The clubs formed part of my early armoury, but the balls, kept out of sentiment, were never used. Even by the standard of the smiling Spitfires and Blue Spots lashed with erratic frenzy throughout my boyhood, they were decrepit. Why, they didn't even have proper dimples.

Years later, from the 5th tee of Whitsand Bay, on top of a 300-foot cliff, they were despatched in rapid succession and with rare straightness, to oblivion in Plymouth Sound after four-putting the 4th.

I never gave these balls another thought, for, truth to tell, they have been followed at irregular intervals and for similar reasons, ever since. But they were brought into sharp and painful focus when I enjoyed a preview of golfing memorabilia to be auctioned by Christie's.

There, neatly parcelled in a plastic bag, was an old ball, just like grandfather's. Older, wiser — and poorer — recognition dawned. These were gutta percha balls which I had launched into the ocean. 'Perhaps £150 each if they were in good condition,' mused Christie's expert, Edward Monagle. 'That's the problem with golfing memorabilia. Most people haven't a clue what they've got.'

One woman, clearing out an attic, found a box of religious tracts which she sent to Christie's. They proved worthless, but among them — in what many would consider appropriate physical juxta-position — was an early golf poem. It fetched around £10,000.

The auctioneers have a similar item: 'The Goff: An Heroi-comical poem', in their catalogue, the sale, which was scheduled to coincide with the Open. Printed in 1793, it was written by an Edinburgh clergyman, Thomas Mathison.

It tells of the city's gentry descending from Edina's towers in quest of fame o'er Letha's plains, but even in those days, the 19th hole had attractions, as Mathison bears witness:

> The vanquifhed hero for the victor fills
> A mighty howl containing thirty gills;
> With noblest liquor is the bowl replete;
> Here fweets and acid, ftrength and weaknefs meet.
> From Indian ifles the ftrength and fweetness flow.

144

Edward Monagle with feathery ball and scared head play club

And Tagus Banks their golden fruits beſtow,
Cold Caledonia lucid ſtreams controul
The fiery ſpirits, and fulfil the howl.
For Albion's peace and Albion's friends they pray.
And drown in punch the labours of the day.

The most recent item for auction is the Open Championship medal awarded to Reg A. Whitcombe, winner in 1938, and one of three brothers who played in the 1935 Ryder Cup team. It was expected to fetch between £4,000 and £6,000.

There is a wooden clubhead, blackthorn with a ramshorn inset, by the St Andrews manufacturer A. Philp, which was expected to fetch from £1,200 to £1,800. New, around 1820, it would have cost 3/6d, or 17½p. In those days the only ball available was the feathery, which cost about 2/6d, or 12½p. It was only the advent in 1848 of the gutta percha, or gutty, which cost about a shilling (or 5p) that brought the cost of the game within reach of the ordinary man.

Now, as I know to my cost, just two of these balls would have left change after paying the annual sub.

FIGURING IT OUT

ELSPETH BURNSIDE

While watching the recent US Open on television, one was aware of continually being bombarded with statistics. Curtis Strange — 35 holes without a birdie; Ian Woosnam — 16 greens hit in regulation.

I've played the game for (whisper it!) 17 years and from the start — just one of my many strange quirks — I have kept a personal log of statistics. The number of birdies, eagles, holes in one (one!) have all been recorded along with other such information as the lowest club needed, each season, to reach the greens at my home club, shots holed from off the green, and the best eclectic score.

I can look back and find, for instance, that since I took up the game in 1972 there has been only one year, namely 1978, when I haven't managed to hole out with a club other than a putter.

Now I don't know why I started keeping records, although the fact that they are kept in a school homework notebook perhaps gives some indication as to what I should have been doing at the time. And this is the first time that I have admitted to this strange addiction in public.

However, in conversation after a recent pro-am, the professional and one of my amateur partners both revealed that they whiled away the time driving home after a round of golf by counting up the number of greens hit in regulation, number of putts etc. 'I do it every time,' admitted the pro.

It made me wonder if all golfers repeat the process. Do we all act like mini computers after every game?

Of course cricketers are famed for keeping a catalogue of runs scored and bowling successes, and footballers often keep detailed accounts of where and when goals are scored. But golf lends itself, even more, to statistical records due to the fact that every shot counts.

For example, while Sandy Lyle may be able to reel off the number of putts in a round, I doubt whether Stefan Edberg knew how many backhand winners he hit in yesterday's match on Wimbledon's Centre Court; or if David Gower was aware of his tally of cover drives in the current Test.

The amount of literature that drops through my letter box from the European Tour headquarters every week would also suggest that golf is a world of paradise for those connected with 'lies, damned lies, and statistics'.

For instance, they informed me that Mark James, in winning the English Open at the Belfry, hit his longest drive 256 yards, hit 77 per cent of fairways in regulation, 69 per cent of greens in regulation and had an average of 27.5 putts per round. And did you know that, for the season, Scotland's Gordon Brand and Stephen McAllister head the 'greens in regulation' rankings with respective averages of 79 per cent and 77 per cent?

The European Tour, under the expert jurisdiction of chief statistician Bill Hodge, has kept similar records for the past seven years. They are produced tournament by tournament by Peter McEvoy's company, Sporting Concepts.

'The pros are all tremendously interested in the figures,' said Angus Gray of Sporting Concepts. 'They all want to know who's done what, and where they stand. Last year we introduced a new category, working out the players' handicaps, and that created a lot of interest.'

So perhaps I'm not so strange after all — maybe all golfers have something resembling my faded blue notebook. Mind you, if my golfing friends now start casting strange looks in my direction I'll know they don't.

INVISIBLE HAZARDS

ANDY MacKAY
Everything was going well, 1 under par at the turn and a long, straight drive up the 10th. A little flick with a No. 6 iron would see the ball on the green and a potentially dangerous hole would be passed with a par logged on the card.

With confidence flowing, a mental picture gave the shot a low difficulty ratio. Prepare to strike: steady backswing, milli-second pause at the top, increase power, through . . . *Sacre bleu!* A s****!

My immaculate vision had been destroyed. Instead of looking up to see the ball hover hawk-like above the green it had chosen a right-angled flightpath before nestling in the roots of a tree.

With my brain scrambled and body aching as though it had suffered an inguinal attack, I tried to reason why this devastating incursion should have occurred. My conclusions were not firm as I finally retrieved the ball from the cup after a 7.

Later, I reasoned that the sudden drop in temperature which followed the shot perhaps indicated the presence of a *spirit* and that my body had been momentarily possessed by one of the non-golfing variety that had left me hooking like mad and in need of a 4 to break 90.

An après-golf clubhouse discussion of the event revealed my experience not to be exclusive. Indeed, it emerged that golfers of all qualities have suffered similar, inexplicable exposure.

Tales of putts no more than seven inches that had mysteriously 'floated over the hole' were all too common, as were accounts of bogey holes where a curse of doom swiftly terminated an unblemished scoring run.

What then can be done to eliminate this extraordinary complication that makes the game more of a chance excursion than one of sheer skill and has been known to cause the gentleman golfer to test the aero-dynamics of his golf club?

Then it struck me. What was required was a lucky charm, an amulet or talisman, a secret ritual or conjuration.

But shivering hickories, is it not the case that we golfers are a superstitious lot? What had been missing in my equipment others had, and had been secretly practising for years.

Observation of golfers provides incontrovertible evidence. How often is it so easy to recognise someone on the course because they always wear the same colour of clothes? Those pretty little Noddy hats with the occasional colourful pom-pom are worn with unashamed enthusiasm. And just look at the rituals that are exercised by some before hitting that tiny wee ball. Some take three practice swings, others as many as seven, often followed by a little waltzing Matilda before the head wobbles to a halt and a final forward, backward or sideways lunge completes the vital exercise.

It is not just club golfers who pursue these secret manoeuvres to gain maximum advantage? Leading professionals are also prone to odd behaviour.

Jack Nicklaus always puts on his left shoe first and never plays with the same ball for more than two holes — and that isn't because it is liable to explode with the crushing blows he administers.

Gary '200-press-ups-every-morning' Player will not play with odd-numbered balls and indeed has a preference for No. 2. And Seve Ballesteros refuses to play with a No. 3 ball because he feels it encourages him to three-putt. This kind of behaviour has been going on for generations.

Simple swinger and five times Open champion Peter Thomson has had an attachment with a loop of elephant hair and has eaten Indian herbs while chanting Chinese magic words to see him through tournaments.

Prior to the start of a Ryder Cup match at Muirfield a public affirmation of superstition was witnessed by many when Nicklaus and Tom Weiskopf were paired together. Weiskopf will not leave the tee without having three dimes in his pocket and he had turned up with only two. He frantically appealed for a dime from someone, but Jack Nicklaus could not resist making light of his partner's anxiety. Nicklaus later confessed that he, too, always carried three coins in his pocket and when marking the ball he always did so tails up.

There is no escaping for the caddie either. One caddie was instructed by his master to change the ball every three holes. The caddie decided that as his boss was going well he would not change the ball for fear of putting a curse on the remainder of the round. The player, Al

Geiberger, went on to shoot a historic round of 59 in the 1977 Danny Thomas-Memphis Classic.

The better the golfer, it seems, the more chance of succumbing to additional aids — and I thought it was all technique.

I am now fully equipped to face these difficulties in the mind, not the least helped, I might say, by the golf club committee who denied my inspired request for a battery of prayer wheels to be installed at the first tee.

My personal, not-so-secret ritual is that, before going on the course, I face St Andrews and turn around three times. This makes me sufficiently dizzy to hit the ball straight out of bounds. An excellent excuse.

THE SON RISES

DOUG CAMPBELL

I blame my son. 'Let's take up golf, dad!' he said excitedly after watching flashbacks of great golfing moments on the TV. And I, like a fool, agreed, not knowing what I was letting myself in for.

Clubs, ah yes, I had them . . . somewhere. An old uncle had given me a set many years before. 'Who is Tom Morris?' I thought scraping the rust and muck off the heads. Clubs still don't have wooden handles — do they?

Right! Santa was good to the lad, forking out nearly £100 for a half-set of clubs bearing the name of Bernhard Langer. All we need now is a few lessons from a reputable professional, and we're away.

It's great working on the *Herald* sports desk as I do. Everyone plays golf, and they are all keen to help two poor innocents starting out.

'Hold the club like this,' said the Chief Sub-editor, picking up a ruler and holding it between his palms, and his pipe between his front teeth. 'Just wrap your hands around the shaft like this. It's easy.' Smoking tobacco cascaded from the pipe almost burning me, but I got the message. Easy eh! Why then was he explaining to someone else that he had 'played like an old woman' over his beloved Haggs Castle course that very afternoon?

But my colleagues agreed to a man that lessons were the only correct course of action we should take. But who? Where?

Living in Kirkintilloch, we were spoiled for choice, but decided that Ken Stevely, the professional at Cawder, was the man for us.

It's a lovely drive up to the clubhouse at Cawder where you have wall-to-wall courses — Keir on the right, and Cawder, known not so affectionately as 'Vietnam', on the left.

'A good professional will sort you out.' I could still hear the good advice ringing in my ears as I opened the door to the pro shop. Two young lads stood there repairing clubs, flanking a big guy who was dressed like Jean-Claude Killy, complete with ski hat.

'I'm Ken Stevely,' the tall man said. 'Can I help you?' So much to do, and I was amazed to understand just how much he could help us in so little time.

After six lessons, I was doing quite well in that I could hit the ball in the general direction I was aiming for, and a fair distance. As for my son, Russell — 'I'll now fade the ball to the left around that tree,' he told me. Sure enough, that is what happened. And this from a boy who had not even held a golf club before the pro's tuition.

'A golf club, we must join a golf club,' I thought. The obvious one was Kirkintilloch, and, to my surprise, I was accepted quite quickly, but not the lad. His name was placed on a waiting list, for how long I do not know. I can take him on 12 times per year, but it does seem daft that young players, who are keen on the sport and whose names are on a club's waiting list, are restricted to a mere 12 visits per year when accompanied by a parent who is a member.

However, there we were, standing on the 1st tee at Kirkie. By now we both had new clubs, I had a new bag and trolley. To pot with the expense I thought, as three elderly women members arrived near the tee.

The pro's figure was standing in front of me, in my mind at any rate, and now was my big moment.

Ball lined up correctly? . . . yes! Feet not too far apart but in line with the target . . . check! Now slowly back and drive for the hole. Everything felt great. I made good contact with the ball but where did it go? 'Did you see it Russell?' I asked my son. 'It went over on to the other fairway,' he replied.

'You don't mind if we play through?' a female voice from behind inquired.

I wanted to go home there and then. 'Stupid damn game, golf. I could be enjoying myself, having my teeth drilled or something like that,' I thought trudging over on the 18th fairway in pursuit of my ball.

Is there any other sport that brings you down to earth with such a great bump? One hole putting for par, the next trying to keep in single figures.

However, I have persevered and now have been playing for six months, and, after a refresher course from Ken Stevely — and lots, lots more practice — I hope to see my name well up there in the *Herald*'s Parbusters chart before long.

FOOT SOLDIER'S TALES

JOHN DUNCAN

We perambulated gently to Troon in a borrowed bullnose Morris. The Palmer swing proved rather quicker, certainly just as robust.

He won the 1962 Open by a street. The car seemed to go home on the pavement. A new philosophy was created in our club.

'Hit it high and watch it fly' was the consensus gleaned partly from the obvious violence of the swing, partly from Palmer's written (ghosted?) advice to belt the ball out of sight first, then learn to ask questions about technique. Most of my vintage still fail in this endeavour.

At this time, however, it was glorious and it was American-style. Had not Palmer already charged to umpteen victories on American television in an era when prime-time advertisements allied themselves to General Custer's birdies and bogeys? Had he not shaken hands with a Cleveland lawyer called Mark McCormack in a deal which was to revolutionise the commercialising of the sporting world? Had not a decade passed since the austere machine Hogan triumphed at Carnoustie on his single Open appearance?

Youth is impressionable. Palmer, the finest sporting ambassador America has produced since questions were first asked about the Atlantic alliance, set about bludgeoning the course — and incidentally British golf — into shape with a gusto which will forever stick in the memory. He hit the ball pretty hard too.

The first time I followed A. P. he was attempting to *qualify* for the 1960 Centenary Open at St Andrews in his initial round on the New Course. He did so with ease and a singular lack of timber ('What's a one-iron?'), from the tee. Eventually, of course, he lost by one shot to Kel Nagle, a Lochgelly-leathery Australian who disconcertingly addressed every shot from the shank of the club. Like MacArthur, Palmer returned.

Two years later at Troon he played possibly the best 72 holes of his life, a 276 total, eclipsing the field with an unfailingly courageous array of strokes, particularly on the greens. Birkdale in a gale in 1961 had already established the presence.

'Go get 'em, Arnie!' rang round the golfing world. That was the message in the sky. To join his Army, then, when recruits colossally outnumbered conscripts, was to march on Georgia, Southport, Troon, Tokyo (Arnie's teahouses) or Timbuctoo, in the certainty of magnanimity in victories (many) or defeats (also glorious).

The outrageously ungainly slings from the tee could for the moment successfully confront the nuclear arsenal of the youthful Nicklaus. It was American; it was war; it was fun; and it taught the rest of us a superb lesson.

SHIVER ME LIVER

BILLY PIPER

Shafts of evening sunlight had just entered the gentlemen's lounge overlooking the 18th green when the glass of rich brown Amontillado reached the Oldest Member's lips . . . and stopped.

'Anything wrong?' inquired the young man who had been standing at the bar.

'Good God. Heavens above. Oh my word. What, what, what does that young man think he is doing?' asked the Sage.

'Putting out by the looks of it.'

'Yes, but, but, but . . . what is that attire?'

'Oh, I see, yes. Well, er, the bottom half is covered in jeans and on the upper half is something called a sweatshirt.'

'But the chap's improperly dressed,' blurted the Oldest Member.

'Not since last week, Sir. The committee changed the rules. It seems some of the good young players were talking about moving clubs because our dress rules were too stiff.'

In an unprecedented scene the Oldest Member emptied his glass in one gulp and sat down muttering.

'Are you sure you're all right, Sir?' inquired the man.

'Yes, yes. All right now. Just a bit shocked you know. I remember the time . . .'

With as much diplomacy as he could muster, the younger man said, 'Well, actually, Sir, I must be . . .'

'Now what year was it? Let me see . . . must have been '32 or perhaps '33.'

'I'm sorry, I'm afraid I shall have to . . .'

'No, it was definitely '34. I remember exactly now because that was the year old Sam Postlethwaite took 25 to get out of the bunker behind the 17th. Finally went round in 168. Twice his age. Not bad, eh?'

The new man sat down and sighed: 'Oh, well, I suppose I can spare a few minutes.'

The Oldest Member warmed to the task of recollection. 'Notice I said bunker. Not this stupid sand trap nonsense. Heard a chap on the wireless the other day referring to something called a putting surface. I ask you? What's wrong with a green?'

'It's the influence from the colonies, you know. All these damned Yanks and Aussies. All right, they can play a bit, but why don't they speak English and dress properly instead of looking like streaky rainbows?

'I remember when a jacket, tie, plus-twos or fours, a good stout pair of brogues and a tweed cap were the order of the day. Smart dress, smart play, I always say.

'A chap tried to come in here after eight o'clock the other evening without a tie. Wearing something called a polo neck he was. I ask you? A polo neck. Chap ought to go and see the club doctor. It sounds like a complaint.

'Talking of complaints. I've complained to the committee about all these long rounds. Five hours for a round of golf. Ridiculous. I watch a pal teeing off from the 1st and have a few G and Ts waiting for him to come down the 18th and it costs me a fortune, besides playing havoc with the old liver.

'I remember, in my youth, playing 72 holes in a day and still having time to catch a tram into town to see George Formby at the Palace Theatre.

'As for these intrusions called carbon shafts, metal woods, irons and so on . . . whatever happened to the brassie, mashie, niblick, spoon and, my favourite, the Gentleman's Persuader?

'I'd like to see these whipper snappers play well if they had to tee up a gutty on a bit of sand and give it a good cuff with a hickory, eh, what? That would soon sort out those with the knack and those who play like a lass in a long frock. Now there's another subject . . .'

While the Oldest Member pondered this new train of thought the man saw his chance.

'Sorry, but I will have to go. I'm afraid that was my young boy we saw on the 18th. He's off scratch, you know, and I think he's just broken the course record.'

As the Oldest Member was helped into the ambulance he was heard to mutter repeatedly: 'Scratch, jeans, course record, sweatshirt. Impossible — never!'

With sincere apologies to P. G. Wodehouse.

THE LONG HOLE

One of P. G. Wodehouse's famous golf tales was acted out by Ballochmyle 6-handicapper Jimmy Thomson, who played seven miles cross-country between Cumnock and Ballochmyle.

With ball-spotters taking up advance scouting positions, Jimmy, using a full set of clubs, played across the A76, the River Lugar and a railway line. He also had to vary his route when he found that three fields had been unexpectedly planted with barley. Naturally, a score was kept and the 'hole' was played in 108 strokes, averaging about 115 yards a shot.

Unlike Wodehouse's story in which two golfers and rival suitors played for the hand in marriage of a young woman, Jimmy was playing to raise funds for Cumnock rugby club.

HACKERS' CHARTER

BILL SUTHERLAND

One hears golfers say: 'So-and-so just hacks round in about 102.' Hacks? 102? That's pretty good shooting if you ask me.

When on holiday in Largs at the age of 12, I went round the Routenburn course in 192. I had begun in sunny weather, but there was a thunderstorm by the turn. It *was* the same day, I should add. Thereafter the symbolism of a bright start giving way to gloom at the furthest point from the clubhouse has dogged my footsteps like a sullen caddie. A round of golf for me is like a sad version of *King Lear*.

Years later I managed a 147 there, a score I would rather have emulated on the snooker table. The family record for Routenburn is claimed by my brother, who brags that he once shot 121. But he had no witnesses, so I suspect a bit of cheating.

In between my attempted comebacks, I contented myself with playing on a hilly nine-hole course in the south side of Glasgow, where the short but uphill 4th hole convinced me that the course designer had been born and brought up on the North Face of the Eiger.

The so called green at that time was a patch of the fairway where the grass had been cut almost imperceptibly shorter. I once was on in 4 and went on to take some 20 putts, each (bar one) tracing out a cruel parabola, arcing past the hole, and trickling to an equidistant spot. Why did I persevere? Well, I wasn't going to pick up and just give in; no sir, not after having hit the green in only 4, for goodness' sake.

I have continued to find golf to be an uphill struggle ever since, and it is clear that only this drastic revision of the rules can give us hackers an even break.

1. **Par** — The standard score for every hole should be (rounded up) half the square of the present par. That would allow you 5 ('half' of 9) at the short holes, 8 at the par-4s, and 13 strokes for all those safaris where it takes me the allocated 5 just to hit the fairway. The present par of 72 for courses with, say, three short and three long holes thus would be revised to a much more sensible 150.

2. **Lost Balls** — Logic insists that if it costs you two strokes for losing a ball, you should deduct two for finding one. I would even subtract three shots if the ball you find is in good condition, i.e. there are still some dimples on it.

3. **Hazards** — At the player's option, he or she could dispense with using a club. The player would be permitted to retreat from a hazard and choose whether to throw, kick, or otherwise propel the ball in the direction of the hole. Or in any direction, for that matter.

4. **Preferred Lies** — Once per hole, instead of having to play the ball from where it lands, you could place it on the spot where you meant it to land; except, of course, on the green. Some cheats would always try to make out that that was where they really had intended the ball to go. You know the types.

5. **Other Rules** — All existing rules of golf would be abolished as being unnecessary (e.g. simply plain commonsense), or incomprehensible, or just daft.

Already golf is like a game of snakes and ladders, without the ladders. The rules only compound your misery.

'Serves you right,' the heartless rules seem to say. 'Moreover, now that your ball has landed on this five-foot square island, with your lie being a mixture of slate, bamboo grass, and loam, you may use only your putter for the 150-yard carry over water back to the mainland. And another thing: because of the sand content in the loam, you must not, of course, ground your club. PS: Remember to rake over the sand and/or replace any divots.' It's rather like asking you to wipe up the blood after you have been guillotined.

Contrast that with the words of sympathy which the new rules would convey:

'Jolly bad luck, Sir/Madam. But welcome to Hooker's Island. Isn't the scenery lovely? Of the options available we recommend invoking the preferred-lies rule. Good luck with your next shot, and have a nice day.'

Look at it this way, fellow hackers, if anyone wants to go round in 99, 75, or — perish the thought — under 70 for a par-150 course, that's up to them. Let them waste their money. We par-hackers will always have more hits per round, so we obtain much better value.

TURNING THE TIDE

DAVID STEELE

A subject dear to this heart, and hopefully to many others who daily pursue excellence while attaining mediocrity on the golf course, is the conservation of the ground on which we play this marvellous game.

(Relax, dear reader, you are not about to be lectured on the ozone layer or be treated to an essay on the effects of acid rain. Not for this correspondent the quest for a Green Britain as so hideously practised by vote-seeking politicians in recent times.)

The best example for any discussion on golf is usually one's own club, and in this case, it is no different. The 138-year-old links at Prestwick St Nicholas are under attack from the sea.

Sadly, King Canute is not on the committee, so the old chap cannot be sent down to turn back the tide, would that he could. Instead, the members currently fulfilling that most vital yet least appreciated function of all, God bless them, are left in a quandary.

The waters of the Firth of Clyde do not always lap, azure blue, against the sand as they have done in recent weeks. Instead, for many months of the year they thrash against the boundaries of our much-loved stretch of golfing land and are having a good go at depriving us of some of the best holes.

By now the testing part at the far end of the course would have disappeared if it had not been for our friends from the roads department who dump the stuff they have no more use for on the stretch between the course and the beach.

Yet there are murmurings that this will have to stop. The roads chaps are not playing the game and all sorts of nasty boulders, clods of earth and assorted debris of an unwelcome nature are finding their way on to this corner near the Newton shore.

It was never, with the best will in the world, Bondi Beach along this part of Ayrshire, but it has become really quite unpleasant in recent times and something will have to be done.

If it is a choice between a scruffy bit of beach, though, and the absence of the holes between the turn and the 13th tee, well . . .

Happily it seems that common sense will prevail and the committee are about to have chats with the regional council on the whole question of dumping. They have a powerful ally in local member John Baillie, who has said he would push for a permanent solution to the problem, perhaps in the form of those baskets filled with giant chuckies that you see at the side of by-passes.

He is keen to give his constituents a better beach on which to wander and although he is not a golfer (does he know the joys which are being missed?), he has a sneaking regard for those among us who are.

It has been a delight to be associated with St Nicholas over the past few years and while the moans may resound around the clubhouse — as they do wherever golf is played — there has never been a guest of mine who has left the place with less than great memories of the course and the après-golf.

The only thing which rankles a shade with this golfer is the growing problem of dogs on the course, which the committee seems powerless to do much about. The solution lies instead with the otherwise sound and God-fearing people of Prestwick.

It really is hard enough to choose a club, line up, and perform a shot which will extricate the infernal pill from the rough and propel it in the general direction of the green without having to contend with canine excrement.

One moment to savour came in a match with three celebrated journalistic colleagues, when the dulcet tones of one sounded from the right of the 12th hole — near the dumping ground of earlier paragraphs.

'What do you do when your ball is lying on a dog's turd,' quoth the sporting scribe. 'Sounds like a loose impediment, play it as it lies,' echoed the reply from even his kindly-disposed partner.

A joke's a joke, folks, and we really do not mind the odd dog being walked along the edge of the course, but the best part of a century-and-a-half of golfing tradition deserves better than being used as a grand doggy loo.

At all events, it is a great place to play golf and with a wee bit of fore-thought and common sense on everyone's part it will remain that way for at least another 136 years.

BANDIT COUNTRY!

DAVID BRYDEN *travelled as a guest of Hennessy Cognac to their clubs' championship in Sardinia . . . and found terror among beauty for the handicap golfer.*

A narrow sward of fairway stretched between granite rock and shrub for about 200 yards where bunkers lay on the right and water along the left bit deeper ready to swallow even the slightly off-line tee shot.

Water also guarded the front of the green, while beyond, further banks of bunkers lay in wait for those who got the line right but the distance wrong.

There was a magnificent mountain backdrop to this sight which, despite its splendour, terrified the long-handicap player — and, in the distance, an emerald sea glittered in the Sardinian sunshine. This was the spectacular Pevero course on Sardinia's Costa Smeralda — a millionaire's paradise frequented by the likes of Jackie Onassis — and created by one of the richest men in the world, the Aga Khan.

And 16 amateur players from Scotland, England, and Ireland, and their club pros got a taste of the good life as qualifiers for the final of the Hennessy Cognac Clubs Championship. It was a trip no one is likely to forget — especially John Cook and 7-handicapper Mark Farina of Kenley, who beat Ballater's Fraser Mann and club champion Jim Hardie for the title in a sudden death play-off.

But everyone was a winner by just being there in the golfers' paradise designed by Robert Trent Jones. The great man himself once said: 'Golf offers much more than a perpetual battle between man and setting. Just to be out there, to walk and enjoy natural surroundings is almost enough by itself.' And it certainly was at this course on the 'emerald coast' of breath-taking vistas and air filled with the fragrance of herbs and flowers.

There were wonderful holes on this exacting 6,400-yard test of golf. John Cook, winner of the English Amateur championship at 19 and a Gary Player protégé who enjoyed tour success in the Nigerian Open, described it as the most difficult course he had ever played. Everyone concurred.

Wise-cracking Jim Hardie spoke of playing the *arriverderci* ball. 'One hit and it's *arriverderci!*' Dense shrub inhabited by lizards and the odd four-foot-long black snake (harmless, they said) skirted the tight fairways to punish shots that on other courses would have finished in semi-rough. And there was no shot back as the ball was usually lost, or if found was almost certainly unplayable. Losses in some cases reached double figures in a single round. Fortunately, a trip to the bundi often resulted in a few finds to compensate.

In the Italian Open of 1978 only three players managed to break the 300 barrier in the four-round aggregate — and afterwards in giant reeds at the tough 8th hole, greens staff found some 800 balls!

So this Hennessy Sardinian shoot-out favoured the partnership of club pro and bandit.

And I have to say that the way some of the 7 and 8-handicappers hit the ball was not bettered by more than a few of the pros.

Former Ryder Cup player Brian Waites expected a lot from his 8-handicap partner. At one hole the Notts pro did some pacing, looked at his yardage chart and said: 'It is 87 yards to the pin. Hit between a ¾ and ⅛ wedge.' That is really pinpointing the target!

So the amateur learned that accuracy is paramount. Playing the iron for position is often the best policy when one is tempted to go for distance with wood . . . certainly the case at Pevero. But there is still a place for those with a dash of adventure. Jim Hardie proved that as he continually played wood to great effect where the pros proceeded with more caution.

While Jim and Fraser Mann were keeping Scotland to the fore on the course, our other representatives, Erskine's Peter Thomson and Bob Haswell, who found it tough going as a team, were still great ambassadors for Scottish golf and received one of the biggest cheers at the prizegiving.

Now, before those who have sampled the delights of golfing in Portugal, Majorca, the Costa del Sol, and Tenerife think of taking up the Sardinian challenge next year, a word of caution. You will need thousands — that's not lire, I mean pounds in sterling.

We stayed at Hotel Cervo in Porto Cervo, ten minutes' drive from the course (taxi £11 each way). The Citalia brochure this year prices a 14-day stay half-board as high as £2,052 flying out of Gatwick.

Pevero's charges are about £35 a round plus £50 to hire an electric cart . . . and afterwards four bottles of beer at the bar will cost you more than a tenner.

WHO IS THE GODFATHER?

It is the ultimate golfing experience, if you can afford it — and, no doubt, it can be done cheaper. Of course, you could always qualify for the Hennessy finals next year — but that, too, is not easy. A total of 1,009 clubs entered last year's tournament and it is estimated that over 150,000 players took part in club medals in a bid to qualify with their club pro for the regional finals.

It's worth giving it your best shot. *Buona fortuna!*

DECK OF CARDS

TOM SHIELDS

A golfer was sitting playing with a deck of cards in the members' lounge when he was confronted by the secretary of the handicap committee.

'Why are you sitting playing cards when you should be out playing in the monthly medal?' the secretary chided the golfer.

The golfer replied to the secretary, 'I cannot play in the medal today for I have a bad leg. But sit down, have a gin and tonic, and let me tell you about this deck of cards and how it reminds me of my golf.'

This then is the story that the golfer told:

When I look at the ace, I think of the hole-in-one I once scored at the short 1st, and of the enormous number of strokes I had to take over the next seventeen holes in order to ensure that the bar was closed by the time we finished. The two reminds me of the room number of the hotel where I spent my honeymoon and of the practice swing which shattered the overhead light and embedded several of my young bride's front teeth in my favourite 2-wood. The three and four remind me of the day I needed a par 3 at the 18th to beat the club champion in the Summer Quaich and the four putts that I took from four feet. The five reminds me of the number of days each week that women were allowed on the course and I didn't have to carry my own clubs. The six brings to mind Rule 6b in the *Club Handbook* which prevented my wife from entering the members' lounge, and her pleasure when I remembered to take a packet of crisps and a half of shandy out to the car park for her. The seven reminds me of the MacGregor RPM Parabolic Groove 7-iron with New Spaceage High-Modulus Alda HM-46 Graphite and Boron Shaft which I lost when I threw it into the woods at the 14th after it started picking up Radio One. The eight reminds me of the eight rounds a week I had to cut down to after my wife had her wee nervous breakdown. The nine reminds me of part of what Bernhard Langer said when I offered to keep score for him on the practice green before last year's Open. (I didn't fully understand the rest of his reply but it seemed to have something to do with '*eincheekischittzenheader*'.) The ten reminds me of the tender loving care with which I nursed my wife back to golf. The jack, who else but wonderful old Jack Nicklaus — the finest golfer advertising! The queen reminds me of my dear wife and the morning she committed suicide, clubbing herself to death with my Wilson R20 Gene Sarazen Sand Wedge. The grip has never been the same since. The king takes me back to the King's Course at Gleneagles where I was playing in the company's spring outing later the same day — a day which was completely spoiled, incidentally, by a double bogey at the 15th.

The four suits in my deck of cards each have a special meaning for me. The clubs remind me that if you add the numbers of the irons 2 to 9 and the woods 1 to 4, it totals 54 — the age that Peter Alliss was the year before he was 55. The diamonds remind me of my sky-blue Glenmuir sweater which was completely ruined the sad day my dear wife took her life. The spades remind me of my 4-iron than which I would be better using a spade. The hearts make me think of the broken hearts that my late wife's devoted dogs would undoubtedly have died of, if they hadn't been put down, appropriately enough with my Wilson R20 Gene Sarazen Sand Wedge. When I count up the number of spots on my deck of cards, it comes to 365, only one digit different from the Dunlop 65, my favourite golf ball. When I count the number of cards in my deck I find 52 which is exactly the number of strokes it took me to play from the 4th tee to the cemetery on the day of my wife's funeral, including holing out a 90-yard chip shot from behind the cortege. 'So you see,' the golfer finished, 'this deck of cards is both rulebook and scorecard to me.'

A TOUCH OF THE
BIZARRE

Few aspects of golf hold more fascination than the hole-in-one. No golfer can honestly say that, from a distance of 100 yards or more, he is aiming a ball 1.68 inches in diameter to end up in a hole 4.25 inches in width. Statistical analyses have shown that for an average golfer the odds against achieving this are 42,952 to one. Yet information received by *Herald* Club Golf has shown that not only have our intrepid golfers beaten the odds, but they have done so in some unusual circumstances.

At Fereneze, Brian Connolly using a driver at the 18th in the medal finals holed in one. This hole measures 374 yards, and, according to the *Golfers' Handbook*, there are only three longer recorded drives in Great Britain (393 yards at West Lancashire's 7th by Peter Parkinson in 1972, 380 yards at Tankersley Park's 5th by David Hulley in 1961, and 380 yards at White Webbs 12th by Danny Dunne in 1976).

The hole is downhill and the shot was further aided by a following wind and a dry fairway. Nevertheless it must have been a splendid strike by the 17-handicapper who recorded a net 69, his albatross at the last making up for a 9 at the 3rd.

According to the handbook, Brian has a strong claim for having achieved the longest hole-in-one in Scotland. But local intelligence, confirmed by the man himself, informs us that the very same hole was aced 11 years ago by Peter Kinloch of Cardross, using a No. 3 wood, and witnessed by his twin brother Jim who was playing in the match ahead and was on the green when the ball went into the hole.

Our source at Kilmarnock Barassie has told us of two hole-in-one's within four days. The first was in a club match against Royal Troon, when 73-year-old J. B. (Jock) Brown, the former Clyde and Scotland goalkeeper, hit his tee shot at the 220-yard 15th to within two feet of the flag. Barassie were dormie four (four up with four to play) at the time and he remarked to the past captain Jim Torbett, as he played his shot, 'You have that to win the match.' Jim promptly holed his No. 5 iron tee shot and celebrations followed.

Then, while playing in the second round of the club championship, Leslie Crawford, who has won the championship on nine previous occasions, holed in one at the 149-yard 9th. This time, however, his ace proved to be unlucky as he finished runner-up to Jim Milligan in the competition.

The hole-in-one must be the ultimate in golfing perfection whether the ball lands straight in the cup, bounces in, rolls in or, even more spectacularly lands beyond the pin and spins back. There are instances of people holing in one on their first rounds, doing two in successive holes, and holes halved in one. But not all have been achieved by a beautifully crisp shot.

The one by A. Christie at the 159-yard 8th at Carluke during the club's senior open could be described as tree-mendous. A look of dismay followed the ball off the tee. It was heading for the woods. But there were smiles all round when it rattled off the timber, on to the green, and into the ultimate place of rest.

He fails to beat perhaps the flukiest hole-in-one recorded. Ted Bowenhouse shanked his No. 7 iron tee shot on the 145-yard 4th hole at the Mountain View club in Oregon. The ball flew over a barbed wire fence into a field where it bounced off the head of a grazing cow. From there it came back on to the course, landing on a sprinkler head and deflecting off a mower parked at the side of the green, en route to the hole.

Not always when you strike a ball from the tee straight into the hole does it count as a one. In one case we heard of, it went down as a magnificent 7. In a charity foursome at Carluke, 17-handicapper Alistair Bell hit his tee shot at the 147-yard 11th into trees on the right. His partner, Elizabeth Thomas, playing three off the tee, hit her shot into trees on the left. Alistair, playing five, found trees on the right again. None of the three balls were found and Elizabeth trudged back up a hill to play seven off the tee. The foursome behind, now patiently waiting on the tee, then watched in astonishment as she hit the ball sweetly into the cup.

At Westerwood, co-designer Severiano Ballesteros was hitting a dozen balls for the benefit of the media at the par-3 15th, a feature hole on the then incomplete course. Nine of the first 11 made the putting surface, the other two missed on the right, the place he had nominated because he wanted to see what trouble errant shots would find. One ball to go and the Spaniard announced: 'This time a hole-in-one.' The No. 7 iron shot split the pin all the way. 'No kidding, no kidding,' he

100-holes-in-a-day Strathaven trio

said as the ball plummeted on to the green only to hit the base of the pin and bounce some 15 feet away. Further inspection revealed the pin had been stuck in the green like a spear. There had been no hole. If there had . . . well, we will never know.

And now for a hole in zero. In the junior week at Williamwood, 12-year-old Sandy Keith, playing off 36, holed his No. 6 iron second at the par-4 3rd. With his two-stroke allowance that gave him a big net zero. Hard to beat, but possible. A hole-in-one less 2 would give a net minus 1. Heaven forbid, we have yet to hear of one.

At Williamwood's 16th, which borders a railway line, a member sliced his shot which headed like an Exocet missile for the East Kilbride to Glasgow train. The ball rebounded on to the fairway and the lucky player finished with a par.

On the great links of the Old Course at St Andrews, an elderly local was playing with a member of Her Majesty's forces based at RAF Leuchars when a crow swooped and picked up the senior man's ball. Weighed down by its steal, the bird flew off quail high at less than maximum speed. The young RAF man saw his chance and presumably, using his knowledge of flight patterns, set off in pursuit. Golfers on adjoining holes watched in amazement as the RAF man closed the gap. After some 300 yards, the crow took a look round, sized up the situation, and to great applause from around the links, dropped the ball which was replaced without penalty on the grounds it had been moved by an outside agency.

Did you hear about the Irishman who took 7 to hole out from 18 inches on the final green at Paisley? Bob Wilson, a 9-handicapper, known as Irish Bob to distinguish him from another member of the same name, hit two fine woods to set himself up for a birdie at the 444-yard hole. His first putt was 18 inches short — and he missed that as well. He threw back his head in anguish, covering his eyes with his hands, and accidentally kicked the ball almost off the green. The two-stroke penalty — he thought — was followed by four more putts, the first two charged past the hole in anger. 'Oh, woe is me,' Bob was overheard to remark as a 10 was marked on his card. As if that was not enough, David Miller from Milngavie, looked up the rule book and told us the following week: 'As he did not replace his ball after kicking it, he should have been disqualified. The penalty which he incurred was, incidentally, one stroke and not two (Rule 18-2a(i)).'

Cleanliness is next to Godliness, so the saying goes. In that respect make what you will of this story heard at St Andrews from lawyer Sandy Tatum, former president of the United States Golf Association, who is a member of the San Francisco Golf Club where he is one of those responsible for introducing an English Day there. Two conditions exist for those taking part. The first is that the format is

David Begg stops the watch as John Chillas sinks the final putt in a 14-minute round

foursomes. Fair enough. The second is that participants are forbidden to take a shower afterwards!

A Glasgow golfer, who shall be nameless, was in hospital for an operation to remove a varicose vein from an extremely personal area of his anatomy, and was anxious about his fitness for a forthcoming outing. 'What are the chances of me being able to play golf in a fortnight?' he asked the operating surgeon, himself a golfer. 'Well,' came the reply, 'it depends on how the ball lies.'

ROUND IN A FLASH

Traditionalists believe a round of golf should never take more than three hours, but there is a body of golfers who hold the opinion that anything longer than a quarter of an hour is pretty slow.

The perpetrators were Tartan Golf, at Newbattle in March 1989, when they launched their new spring catalogue during an open day involving 160 golfers, 42 of them professional. Before serious play

165

began, an effort was made to beat either the world record for manoeuvring a ball round a course of 9 minutes 51 seconds, set in South Africa in 1988, or the unofficial Scottish record of 14-33.

The technique was to put a professional on each tee on the 6,012-yard course, and on strategic fairway points to give the best chance of a good drive and approach shot. The amateurs, including yours truly, were on and around the greens with the task of holing out and providing an express delivery of the ball for the next tee shot. Only the time was important. The score was immaterial which was perhaps just as well.

A first attempt was aborted after a ball was lost, but it gave a taste of the exercise. Progress of the ball could be made out by the sight of scurrying golfers. The standard of some of the shots, particularly the amateurs, was questionable and included a rapid-fire Hamlet job by one poor soul, who almost emptied a bunker.

The world record was not remotely approached, but a new Scottish record of 14 minutes 18.61 seconds, an average of 45 seconds per hole, was established at the second attempt, Stirling professional John Chillas, who had set the ball in motion, holing the final putt to delirious scenes as organiser David Begg pressed the button on the stopwatch.

Beneficiaries of the exercise were Erskine Hospital and Forth Charity Trust.

ROUND...AND ROUND...AND ROUND

Those who think 36 holes in a day is tiring should spare a thought for three juniors from Strathaven — Mark Keder, Grant Nisbet, and Greig Wilson — who completed a dawn-to-dusk target of 100 holes, more than five rounds, three-and-a-half hours ahead of schedule. They tallied 1,381 shots — 131 in excess of their target — and raised more than £600 for junior club funds in the process.

They began at 4.30 a.m., and later in the day seniors kept ahead of play urging others to let the boys through without delay. Some players, in fact, allowed the boys through twice in the one round. They finished at 6.30 p.m.

THE LYON ROARS

Bizarre tales from the past are coming to light as club historians delve into the archives to produce centenary publications. Two such are *Golspie Golf Club 1889-1989*, by Rod Houston (£2, plus £1 postage and packing) and *Dunaverty Golf Club, The First Hundred Years,* by Angus MacVicar (£1.50 plus postage).

One story from Dunaverty just before the turn of the century concerns Jimmy Lyon, a thin-faced Glasgow man with a wispy moustache who was dispatched to the southern end of Kintyre in an effort to get him off the drink. His brilliant play brought him the club championship three years out of four, but success was not the only thing that went to his head.

On frequent visits to the Argyll Arms, he would boast, as legend has it: 'When I'm sober, I can see the hole like a flower-pot. Give me two drams and I can see it like a bucket.' It is even said that for a bet, he once drove a ball over the Ugadale Arms Hotel from the face of a watch.

However, his health deteriorated, and he and the captain's prize for club champion of 1898, a ram's horn mounted on silver presented by D. MacCallum, disappeared. Lyon was never seen again, but the trophy was found 16 years ago in a Glasgow antique shop. The MacCallum-Lyon Trophy is now an annual handicap match-play competition.

The shore features largely in the history of Golspie, a strip of land which has been under attack from the Dornoch Firth since the beginning. Occasionally, the shore has been a boon. Witness the experience of James Macpherson, a notable hooker of the ball, in the Golspie Open of 1977. After a tie for first, Macpherson went into a sudden death play-off. At the 4th extra hole, he twice hooked on to the beach only to see the ball take a spurious bounce back on to the course on each occasion, helping him to a par 5. He won at the 7th extra hole.

SINISTER LINKS
WITH SHINTY

Let us take a trip back through the mists of time to Ireland, let's say around 50BC. It's a summer's evening on the northern coast and here we find Cuchullin, that great Homeric Gaelic legend, and a few of his pals heading out to the seaside for a game of *cluiche poill* (the hole game). Cuchullin, as the best player, has the honour and with his curved stick he hacks up a bit of turf and places a wooden ball on top. Checking the breeze coming in off the sea he aims slightly right and then, with an in-to-out swing, draws his shot into the wind. The ball lands a few feet short of a small hole, bounces gently and rolls just past. His opponents, usually happy if they reach this spot in two, view each other with dismay. Yet another defeat beckons. 'We would have a better game if we each had a stroke at this hole,' says one, in Gaelic. Cuchullin, always on the lookout for a fresh challenge, generously agrees, and *cluiche poill* thereby develops a stage further.

Much of this could well be a load of bull, but evidence has just come to the fore suggesting that Cuchullin was the first truly great golfer, and if you accept this, the history of golf, proliferated in just about every book on the game, can be rewritten. Golf was invented neither in Scotland nor Holland but in Ireland and the distant home of the game in this country is not St Andrews but on the west coast, probably Kintyre. Machrihanish would be a good bet. Cuchullin, the Ulster traveller and warrior whom the mountain range on Skye is named after, first excelled at the stick-and-ball game of *camanachd*, now known as shinty in Scotland and hurling in Ireland. But according to a 12th-century book written in Gaelic, the *Book of Leinster*, he was also a master at *cluiche poill*, which sometimes took the form of a player defending the hole from shots delivered by opponents. At other times groups of two or more simply attempted to strike a stationary ball into the hole.

Roger Hutchinson, author of *Camanachd! The Story of Shinty* (Mainstream, £9.95), says such stories cannot be dated exactly. 'They may predate the birth of Christ, or they may be as young as the 12th century. In *cluiche poill*, they provide the earliest clues as to the origins of golf,' he writes.

The view is supported by 19th-century sports historian, the Reverend Charles Rogers from Fife, who described shinty as 'a primitive description of golf, and not improbably its pioneer'.

Camanachd, and possibly *cluiche poill*, were brought to Scotland around the sixth century by Irish Gaels, along with Christianity and the Gaelic language, and there is evidence to show the game spread throughout the country from Galashiels to Aberdeen. At St Andrews University in the 15th century there is a reference to students 'setting aside all superfluities'.

Although no further details of these superfluities are given, Hutchinson commented: 'If shinty was not played at St Andrews at that time it would be very odd because the game was everywhere else.' Certainly, by the 17th century, Hutchinson says, it was clear that at Aberdeen University the two main outdoor sports were shinty and golf.

It is tempting to imagine a big game of shinty being played the full length of the now Old Course at St Andrews prior to the innovation of *cluiche poill* and then golf as happened at other places like the island of Colonsay on a low hill called Cnoc nan Gall (Hill of the Stranger), where shinty was played until last century before the ground became what is now Machrins Golf Course.

By the same token, shinty was played at the Machair Ionain (Shinty Links) on what is now part of Machrihanish Golf Course. Given that this was close to the probable landing point of the first Irish Gaels, Machrihanish could, at a stretch, claim to be the place where golf was first introduced to Scotland.

There is even lexicographical evidence. In an account of an early shinty match at Machrihanish, at the start of the game the ball was placed on a *cogy*, the Lowlands word for a golf tee.

Hutchinson does not push the point, even although he does say the circumstantial evidence of a direct link is strong, preferring to compare the development of the game as being like the evolution of man: the same things happened independently all over the world. Why else would there be a 1930s account of a stick and ball game on the shores of — New Guinea?

A familiar occurrence at Newtonmore Golf Club is for visitors to feel disorientated. Almost half the members there play left-handed, literally a sinister situation. The club has frequently hosted the Scottish Left-Handed championship in which right-handers are ruled out of bounds.

The position is similar in the clubs at Kingussie, Muir of Ord,

Strathpeffer, Oban, Fort William, Glencruitten, Sconser, and Kyles of Bute, where they may try to tell you the phenomenon is a sign of intelligence. That might or might not be the case but the most widely accepted explanation is shinty.

The event is organised by the Scottish section of the British Left-Handed Golfers, formed 30 years ago by American Freddy Ritz and Englishman John Turner, and often attracts more than 60 entrants.

Golf in these northern parts of Scotland exists on a different plane. Theories held the world over are turned upside down and inside out. Shinty, it is claimed, has been played for more than 2,000 years — far longer than golf. So why should it not be that golfers so steeped in history play with grips and swings that would make Harry Vardon turn in his grave?

The explanation goes like this: in right-handed golf the left hand and arm is where the power comes from and the right hand is used principally to guide the club. Logically then, a right-handed person should play golf left-handed. There are two reasons why this generally does not happen.

By far the majority of equipment is right-handed and secondly, professionals tend to teach the game that way. In the aforementioned parts of the Highlands, however, youngsters learn their shinty first and golf second.

It quickly becomes second nature for children to hit the ball both ways, an essential shinty skill. Then, faced with the choice of which way to play the one-sided game of golf, most opt for the left even although they are naturally right-handed.

To confuse matters further, former Newtonmore champion and the club's most successful player, John Wilson, who used to be a shinty goalkeeper, plays cross-handed with right-handed clubs. That is left-hand below right swinging right to left, the method used by many shinty players for taking free hits. You don't find that technique in many instruction books. But it works so why change it?

The shinty swing, whether right or left-handed, often has a further peculiarity in that it tends to be extremely body hugging — up-and-down with a late wrist break. The reason for this is the cleek which, if you performed it on a golf course, would get you thrown off but which is perfectly legal in shinty. An opponent is allowed to obstruct the downswing with his own stick. A wide, flat swing would, of course, make you easy prey.

Shinty does not explain the existence in North America and the Antipodes of left-handers whose natural champion is New Zealand's Bob Charles, the only left-hander to win the Open (1963 at Lytham), and who accepted an invitation from Newtonmore six years ago to play an exhibition match to mark the opening of their new clubhouse. But the theory that shinty gave rise to golf has a distinct appeal which the idea of Dutchmen importing the game to St Andrews does not.

ON THE DISTAFF SIDE

A common male view of women golfers is that they are mostly middle-aged to elderly duffers who hold up play by taking too much time and moving far too slowly between their appalling shots. We even have heard of women who attach knitting counters to their trolleys, a useful device when scores per hole go into double figures.

Although this is probably a prejudicial outlook, women club golfers are the poor relations. With the exceptions of Lundin Links Ladies', who manage their course and clubhouse, and Troon Ladies', who have an independent organisation, Scotland's 34,000 women golfers are attached to men's clubs, have restricted hours of play, and generally have no say in how things are run.

Scottish golf traditionally is a bastion of male domination, with many clubs boasting men-only bars, and in some extreme cases, men only. Full stop. Yet there are signs that the pattern is changing.

In the mid-1970s, the St Andrews-based Ladies' Golf Union reckoned that 50 per cent of women golfers were over the age of 50, but this figure is dropping, a trend due in no small part to the successes of our women professionals, and the Curtis Cup team. Joan Lawrence, the Dunfermline-based former chairman of the LGU, and former Scottish cap and Curtis Cup player, said there was an increasing number of clubs, like Dunblane, which have women on club committees.

'More and more clubs are taking women on to their committees, although they are still a minority. The main argument against is that ladies generally pay only half to 75 per cent of the subscriptions. I think ladies would prefer to pay the same as men and have full playing rights, like they do at Aberdour, a position which would benefit good players.'

171

NINETEENTH HOLE
(Scottish version)

Nineteen is more than one too many.
See these bourgeois less-than-gentilhommes
Swill their booze,
Trapped in the endless rounds
Of Celtic generosity
That prove at once their manhood
And their means.

Listen to the vapid tittle-tattle.
No putting of the world to rights,
No forum of the ordinary man,
Exchanging views on harvest, Gulf, or Gulag,
Not even, heaven help us,
Many rounds of golf refought.

The fragile bonhomie wears even thinner
Against the clatter of the one-arm bandits.
Watch the pack bray if a wife
Should phone with some reminder
Of her husband's proper world.
'She's on the phone, she's on the phone,'
They chant, to the tune of 'The Two Gendarmes'
And all the malice of the mob.

The sheepish fellow is reclaimed,
Made brave by taunts.
What kind of mothers
Did these sons have
To turn them so against their womenfolk?
Male chauvinist pigs indeed
(Unfair albeit to the real Chauvin)
Just hear them honk.

Meanwhile at home
A child calls for its daddy,
A wife waits with churning stomach
For the drunk's return.

Club men?
I could club them.

Lesley Duncan

The changes are far short of a revolution, but the march forward is steady. Over the last ten years, the LGU has seen a membership increase of 18,000. With mixed foursomes also on the increase, everything plainly is beginning to knit together. There even could be a few needle matches in store. The purly gates are opening.

There follow, by way of encouragement to younger women golfers, two cases in point.

If anyone at Bishopbriggs golf club was unsure who exactly Janice Risby was, they no longer can be in any doubt. Her name was called no fewer than eight times at the 1989 prizegiving, when she almost wore a path on the clubhouse carpet. A bag marked 'swag' would have been useful.

The 18-year-old prodigy won everything for which she entered, a feat which might not be as difficult to repeat as Bobby Jones's 'impregnable quadrilateral', but nevertheless will take some doing. The dining-room table in the Risby household at one point was groaning under the weight of cups, medals, spoons, and other trinkets of success. Mother Ann, proud of her daughter's achievements, at the same time was grateful that the club called back most of the silverware for safe-keeping.

The booty included the women's club championship, scratch strokeplay title, handicap championship, and foursomes trophy (with Beth Dyer). As if they were not enough, the club added a watch as a memento of the occasion. There was even one club trophy not there because it was needed for the men's prizegiving, the mixed foursomes trophy (with Neil McArthur).

Janice's response to the question of how it was all done was a nonchalant shrug of the shoulders, as if to say: 'It was nothing.' But behind it all was a great deal of hard work in the four years it had taken to reduce her handicap from 36 to 2 after first trying the game on holiday at Port Bannatyne with father Tony.

Apart from one day a week, when she helps out in her father's fruit and vegetable shop, Janice practises both on the limited area at the club, and at the Strathkelvin Driving Range. The Cawder professional, Ken Stevely, has been keeping an eye on technique in lessons arranged through the West of Scotland Girls' and Scottish Junior associations.

'I would like to turn professional in two or three years' time and if I keep on improving and achieve a handicap of plus 2 which I have been advised is the standard I would have to reach.'

The honours continued to flood in. Janice was a member of the winning Lanarkshire County side, won the West of Scotland Girls' Championship at Troon Portland, represented Lanarkshire in a national county event at Woburn in which she came sixth, and received an award from the West of Scotland Girls' Association for being the most improved golfer of the year. She also was a finalist in the *Herald*'s Parbusters tournament.

On occasions when she has played alongside men, her long game has compared favourably . . . watch out Laura Davies.

FRUITS OF VICTORY . . . Janice Risby with her trophies. Back (left to right) — LGU Challenge Bowl, Jubilee Trophy plus small cup in front to keep (scratch stroke-play). Middle — Singles Trophy (handicap match-play). Scratch Trophy from Stars for Spastics tournament, Foursomes Trophy. Front — First Class Medal Trophy, Campbell Medal, Ladies Championship Trophy (and small cup to keep), National Society for Cancer Relief Spoon, watch from club as special award, LGU Spoon, Eglinton Quaich, team prize won at Lossiemouth in partnership with Mhairi McKinlay

Most club golfers spend a lifetime worrying about a straight left arm, a full shoulder turn, cultivating the right tempo, and a hundred other things without ever getting it quite right. Some people, irritatingly, seem to succeed immediately. Take Elaine Robb, for example.

Two months after having taken up the game seriously, in March 1988 she was women's club champion at Colville Park in Motherwell.

There were certain things already going for her. She had been an under-18 and under-21 Scottish tennis internationalist and then went on to become a county squash player. Elaine is regarded as a natural sportswoman and her job as physical education teacher gives her a professional outlook. Therein possibly lies the key.

With her kind of sporting pedigree it would have been unthinkable when her membership came up at Colville Park not to learn proper techniques, even although she had previously enjoyed occasional bashes round the nine-hole public course at Hamilton and at places like North Berwick and Killin on holiday.

As a teacher of sport she was well aware that bad habits can develop when professional advice is not sought at the outset, faults which can be extremely difficult to correct at a later stage. I wonder how many club golfers recognise themselves in this philosophy.

So before taking to the fairways Elaine went to Brian Dunbar, assistant professional at Strathclyde Park driving range, for a series of lessons. She learned the correct grip, swingpath, and turn, even before venturing out on to the course for her first handicap which was 30.

Six handicap cuts in six months brought her down to 13, and a place in the hall of fame that is magazine *Golf World*'s listings of Britain's most improved golfers of 1988.

Before that happened, Dunbar had been so impressed that he warned the then club champion Pamela Connacher that serious competition was in store.

He said: 'Elaine was very much a novice when she came here but in a matter of two or three months something was beginning to adapt. She is obviously sports orientated, possesses natural talent, and clearly has potential.'

The quickness of success came as a surprise to Elaine, who admits that outside her lessons she has never practised. She had taken up golf both as a game for the future and a sport to play in summer, enjoying the fresh air, the company, and, as the legendary Walter Hagen was fond of saying, 'smelling the flowers along the way'.

Why spoil that by becoming obsessed?

The following year Pamela Connacher gained her revenge by winning the club championship for her eighth time. A 7-handicapper, she had triumphed previously in '77, '78, '81, '83, '84, '85 and '87.

The professional scene, still almost exclusively male, is also changing. Scotland's first woman assistant professional in this modern era, Sarah MacLennan at Ballater, has been appointed, and an enlightened view, which is gathering strength, is that within ten years women club professionals will have become commonplace. In America the pattern is well established and in England there are at least three, Vivien Saunders, Chris Langford, and Mickey Walker, all of whom are holding down top club jobs.

Fraser Mann, the professional at Ballater who appointed Sarah, believes that clubs have simply not thought about the possibility.

'Quite a number of professionals have spoken to me about it and I have detected a sense of jealousy that we have a girl trainee,' he said.

Sarah, 21, a local scratch player before turning professional and a former junior international, had previously helped out in the club shop. Mann added: 'Sarah got the job not because she is female, but because she was a good candidate to become a PGA professional. She has lived in Ballater for a number of years and knows the members well. A few were surprised and pleased about it and there has been no negative response. That is because they are getting the right person for the job. It needs go-ahead people like Sarah to show what the possibilities are.'

He believes that because women play an important role in all but the exclusively male clubs, there should be the facility of a woman professional, and with club professionals becoming increasingly busy there will be a need in years to come for more assistants, many of whom will be women. While male chauvinism is possibly one reason why this has not happened already, another is more practical. There are few women candidates available.

If there were, according to Sarah, there would be far more women professionals. 'There are so many opportunities,' she said. 'A third of the membership of most golf clubs is made up of women but not every lady wants to go to a man for lessons — and I have been teaching a lot of men as well.

'The majority of women who make golf their career have tended to go on tour but there is no reason why women should not make a success of being club professionals. I cannot emphasise enough that the opportunities are there,' added Sarah, who advises any girl wanting to make a career of golf to first contact her club professional.

Since leaving school Sarah has had a variety of jobs, including a spell in the Army in officer training at Sandhurst, 'where they thought I would be better at golf,' she quipped. Although she is combining club duties with tournament play, her ambition is to have her own club shop.

While training from grass roots is one way of doing it, there is a further trend of professionals coming off tour and going into clubs. Chris Langford, one of the first women players to turn professional, became, at the turn of the year, the first committee-appointed club professional in Britain in recent years, at Cleveden near Bristol.

'No one was more surprised than me,' says Chris, 'except, perhaps one or two members at Cleveden. I have been teaching a lot of men, some of whom have come from other clubs. There is no reason why a woman cannot do the job. It depends on the club and it is refreshing to find one like Cleveden which integrates men and women. There is no all-men's bar.'

Chris turned professional and competed in America, returning home when the women's European Tour got going in 1979, winning six tournaments between then and 1982. Later she spent two years in sports promotion, a business background which clearly helped her appointment against more than 30 male applicants. She has since appointed a woman assistant and also a male teaching assistant 'to redress the balance'.

She has found that, in addition to teaching women, there are advantages in a woman teaching a man. 'A male professional hits the ball so far that handicap golfers feel they are playing a different game,' she said. 'When I have played with men in pro-ams we tend to hit the ball similar distances and they can relate more to what I am doing. The same applies during a lesson when I am demonstrating a shot.'

Chris also identifies availability of suitable candidates as a drawback because women's golf is far behind the men's in development, their tour having been going for less than ten years. It is now burgeoning.

There is no sign of the top Scottish women like Dale Reid, Muriel Thomson, Cathy Panton, Gillian Stewart, and Jane Connachan ending their successful tour careers, but Chris added: 'When they do come to that stage they would be fantastic candidates for a job in Scotland, or anywhere else for that matter.'

The first woman assistant professional in Scotland is thought to have been Meg Farquhar, who was assistant to George Smith at Lossiemouth in the 1930s. The first woman professional in England is believed to have been Ethyl Wyngate, sister of Sid Wyngate, who was professional at Templenewsham, Leeds.

Herald *Club Golf has sampled first hand the women's professionaH game. Consider this experience:*
Maureen Garner took one look up the fairway, drew the club back slightly beyond the perpendicular, and effortlessly dispatched the ball 200 yards down the fairway with a controlled draw. Her male playing partners had swiped their drives further. Maureen, however, who was to finish joint runner-up in the tournament proper, was the only one to record a par 4.

This was the Bowring Scottish Women's Open pro-am at Cawder. Among amateurs preoccupation with distance is the norm during pro-ams involving men professionals. They hit the ball further than we do and obviously, one thinks, that is a big reason why they score better. Rationalising a woman professional's performance is different. It is more difficult to deceive yourself.

The simple truth is that women professionals are more practised, play within themselves, know what they are doing, and are consistent. In a word, they are professional, and they are good. Who needs distance for the club medal? No longer will I consider it an insult to be told I played like a woman. In fact, I must make an effort to do just that.

Maureen, an Irishwoman, spent two years at St Andrews University and a further two on an American golf scholarship before winning the British women's amateur stroke-play and match-play titles and turning professional in 1988.

The burgeoning tour is giving rise to an extraordinary jet-set lifestyle which might appear glamorous and exciting, but Maureen and her fellow golfers will tell you a different story, one of harsh routine, tiredness, and the frequent need to take weeks off which is sometimes not possible when schedules have been arranged.

Monday is for travel. Tuesday for practice. Wednesday is pro-am, that interface with the amateur game regarded by the women as a fun day and an opportunity for public relations, while Thursday to Sunday is devoted to the real competition. This merry-go-round lasts for 28 weeks between April and November and many of the women will manage only a few weeks off.

Gillian Stewart of Inverness is one of the established professionals, having found sponsorship from Glasgow firm Claremont Business Equipment, an arrangement which eases the pressure by enabling her to afford a regular caddie.

'It is not the glamorous lifestyle that some people think. It is very hard work,' said Gillian. 'Neither is there a great fortune to be made. It costs me between £15,000 and £20,000 to play the tour. If I win, say £25,000, then people might think I am doing well but in fact I am only £10,000 ahead at best and that is before tax. Golf also takes up the whole day. Today, for example, I was at the course at 8.30 a.m. for a short practice before the round and I will not leave the course until 5.30 p.m. Then I will be back at 7.30 p.m. for the pro-am cocktail party which I have to attend.'

Jane Connachan of Royal Musselburgh, another of the Scottish regulars on tour, is successful enough to be able to afford a specialist golf travel firm to arrange her flights and accommodation abroad. 'That is a big help enabling me to concentrate more on my golf. Most of the girls have to make their own bookings,' she said. Although without an overall sponsor, she is supplied with equipment as is Gillian, by the Ben Sayers company, which also provides a car.

With so many countries visited, achieving a steady diet can be problematic, and 24-year-old Jane provides an interesting insight. 'Thank goodness for Italian restaurants,' she said. 'They are in every country and I have found they are the only place where you know what you are eating. I eat lots of pizzas and lasagnes. The exception to this, funnily enough, is Italy, where the food is awful. They seem to have small restaurants which cater only for local tastes.'

While many male professionals on tour are habitual vitamin pill-poppers, Jane has never found the need, although she does occasionally

take a herbal tablet called 'Angus Cactus' which she takes to keep her calm when enthusiasm flags in the middle of the season. 'The reason I take them is that I have spells of feeling very tired. When that happens my concentration tends to go and as a result I make mistakes. Angus Cactus stops me from getting angry.'

It will take a great deal more than Angus Cactus to stop the advance of women in Scotland's golf clubs.

A WOMAN'S PLACE IS IN THE CLUBHOUSE

ERIC WISHART

The fairer sex come in for a lot of stick. Whether it's steering a car or driving a golf ball, men generally do not rate the ability of women very highly. They are second-class citizens on the golf courses and beneath contempt on the roads. Most of the other tasks they are asked to perform in life they seem to manage reasonably well.

As this is supposed to be about golf, let's pass over women's ability behind a wheel for the present and concentrate on their role — or lack of it — in the golf club. They are the ones, I am convinced, who can bring sanity into the running of our clubs. They are sorely needed in the committee rooms around the country to sort out the mess that men have –ismanaged to create.

Take my club, which will be unknown to most of you. For many years, there have been rules governing the use of the various lounges. The main one of these has been beautifully refurbished (it could pass for a swanky restaurant) at immense expense, but for most of the time, it is the private domain of a handful of older members prepared to wear jacket and tie and is out of bounds to casually-dressed members.

The beautiful lounge was referred to as 'the mausoleum' to me the other night by one of the casually elegant younger members. Most Saturday nights, the club steward doesn't even bother to put its lights on — it is ;hat popular. The ladies can make use of it, but only at certain times. Seldom do they bother.

Some clubs I have visited are more enlightened in their approach. For instance, at the Thorpe Hall club near Southend in the south-east of England, where the Bonallack family are members, a similarly-shaped main lounge, when I visited it, was open to men, women and youngsters at any time in any respectable casual gear. The atmosphere there was the best I've encountered, with the mix of youngsters, ladies (some of them quite dishy) and members proving that we can all get on well together — even in a golf club lounge.

It's time, I feel, to change the outmoded thinking of a lot of clubs in Scotland and relax the stuffy rules that are causing immense dissatisfaction among younger members who are not prepared to abandon their normal leisure gear out of working hours. With a fair share of ladies allowed on committee, these changes, I'm sure, would take place. But as the ladies are generally not 'members' — and have little hope of ever achieving full membership — the prospect is remote.

The male-only committees at many clubs are under the impression that they are gifted with the ability to decide on the various items of furniture, carpets, and kitchen equipment (a role they are seldom asked to play in their own home) required for their club. Most do not have the remotest clue what they're about. Even one woman on the committee would make a big difference — and most likely save their club a fortune in the process.

There is, of course, the added bonus that the more time they spend in the clubhouse worrying about the decor the less time they will spend out on the course, but that takes us back to them being rotten drivers.

THE POWER OF
PERSONALITY

The people you meet as a result of playing golf are probably the biggest single attraction of the game. More and more top world-class golfers are turning their attentions to Scotland and stars of other sports turn to golf once their reign is over. They become one of us and loyal to a new discipline even if they fail to master it as well as their first choice. Tradition is important not just at club level, but across successive generations. Clubhouses have become havens for after-dinner speakers, and radio has been tinkered with in golf instruction format as well as television. In all these situations, the fun of the game shines through as witness the following selections of personalities encountered by *He-Rd* Club Golf.

BOXING CLEVER

As a game for all ages, golf tends to attract unlikely stars from other more youth-orientated sports seeking to keep fit once their careers are over. Why else would you find the likes of two Scottish former world boxing champions, Walter McGowan (fly-weight) and Ken Buchanan (light-weight), putting themselves to the test on the fairways?

The pair responded to a Club Golf challenge and took on Jim Reynolds, who covers boxing for the *Herald*, and myself over Lanark, McGowan's home course, which is six miles away from the 10 a.m. rendezvous at his public bar in Carluke, in a match which was always going to have an element of the unpredictable about it.

The stakes were quickly settled, a modest £1 Nassau, but the handicap situation was not resolved until the second green, where

182

McGowan and Buchanan. Joker's wild

McGowan is informed that with his stroke he has gained a half. The remonstration is immediate: 'Stroke! I'm not taking strokes from you. What do you think I am. A poof?' Clearly, a form of Queensberry Rules were to operate. Well, would *you* have argued?

On the 3rd tee, McGowan's next trick is to do an impersonation of Long John Silver while Buchanan is attempting to drive. Buchanan, a member at Monkton Hall, has a peculiar golfing style. He plays cack-handed, left hand below right. Any connection with boxing? 'Yes, I led with the left so it is natural to put my left hand on the club first and then my right hand above it.' McGowan has a more conventional style, except for half a finger which is missing from his left hand. Both hit the ball a country mile.

The double comedy act continues unabated. The clientele from McGowan's bar — Sandy, Jock, and Sam — are acting as caddies (we were one caddie short). An argument breaks out between Walter and Sandy, which is part of the reason why Buchanan is doing a Hamlet job in a bunker. 'Are you blind,' berates McGowan who has been handed his driver for a fairway shot instead of a No. 3 wood.

On the 11th, the two boxers are strolling down the fairway arm-in-arm revealing a more tender side to the natures of two men who have made their names by knocking lumps out of others.

On the next green Buchanan is lying on his stomach trying to hole the ball snooker-style with the wrong end of his putter. On the 10th tee a minor explosion announces McGowan's drive. Closer inspection reveals that he has placed a match with the head positioned on the impact point of his ball, a trick which he claims to have been taught by David Huish, then captain of the British PGA. Could this be the origin of the term match-play?

'What I like about golf is going out on to the course and having a good laugh with my mates,' says McGowan, but things are beginning to change. The match is all square with three to play, and the competition is severe. Did we ever really doubt their instinctive desire to win?

Reynolds rescues the honour of the *Heral*=by holing from off the green at the last. McGowan's birdie putt for victory pulls up just short. The outcome, appropriately, is a halved game, and we decline the suggestion of a return at Gilmour's Gym. It will be on the golf course.

I later caught up with Jim Watt, former world light-weight boxing champion, as a partner in the Fereneze pro-am, which means that *Herald* Club Golf has now traded fairway blows with all surviving Scottish world boxing champions. Jim, a member at Hayston, after having been announced on the first tee, hit a less-than-perfect shot, and quipped: 'If I'd known I was going to do that, I'd have said I was Ken Buchanan.'

All three are now delightfully nutty golfers.

A LEGEND LIVES ON

Andra Kirkaldy, one of the last of the latter-day outspoken, uncouth golf professionals and master of the withering riposte, is a name which conjures up rich images of the early days of the game at St Andrews where he was professional to the R and A. Fifty-six years after his death, however, the legend is still very much alive albeit in a more polite version.

His great granddaughter, Gillian Kellock, has been one of four students on a Robert T. Jones Memorial Scholarship, a one-year exchange arrangement between St Andrews University and Emory University in Atlanta. It is a venture of which Andra would undoubtedly have approved with a remark along the lines 'she's a lucky booger' even although he had a mercurial relationship with Americans.

One of the many great stories attributed to Andra is of the time the

Walter McGowan

Ken Buchanan

R and A dispatched him to the railway station at St Andrews to meet two important visitors from America, accompany them to the clubhouse, and play with them round the Old Course.

Andra had been warned to be on his best behaviour and the only way he could think of doing this was to say nothing. Not a word was spoken on the journey from the station, nor in the clubhouse where the Americans changed for the game. On the first tee a mute Andra played first, and sent a tremendous drive down the fairway. Unable to contain himself any longer he turned belligerently to the bewildered guests and said: 'Noo, beat that ye boogers.'

Yet Andra did make a pioneering trip across the Atlantic in the early part of the century when he played a series of money matches and was held in such high esteem that he was made a Star of Texas, an extremely high state honour. Back in St Andrews he won the respect of princes and peers having played round the great links with the likes of Asquith, Balfour, Earl Haig, and the Prince of Wales.

Another tale concerning Andra was the time he played with the Bishop of London, who found himself in the notorious Hell bunker on the long 14th. He played a superb niblick shot to clear the hazard and then asked Andra what he thought of that. 'When you die,' came the reply, 'I think you'd better take that niblick wi' ye.'

Gillian, who graduated with honours in psychology and spent one of her four years at St Andrews in residence at Andra's old house just outside the town, completed a unique link with the past in following in the footsteps of both her great grandfather and Bobby Jones, a Freeman of St Andrews, whose Grand Slam came four years before Andra's death in 1934.

Jones attended law school in Atlanta and Emory was established by friends in his memory. Gillian was a guest at the US Masters played at the Augusta National club which was developed by Jones.

The family link does not end there. Andra's grandson, Andrew Kirkaldy Kellock, Gillian's father who was aged two when Andra died, came into possession a few years ago of a trophy won by Andra believed to have been in 1895 in a money match in which he prevailed by one hole against J. H. Taylor, the then Open champion.

Because of its history, the pewter trophy could be worth many thousands of pounds, but instead of selling it which was unthinkable, Andrew, a 9-handicapper and past captain of the Bishopbriggs and Ralston clubs, put it up for competition.

Andrew has also been secretary of the Donald Cameron League since 1972. As an extension of the league, the Andra Kirkaldy Cup is now played for annually by past captains of all the competing clubs.

Sadly, Andra, who in his younger days served with the Black Watch in Egypt, never won the Open Championship. The nearest he came was in 1889 when he tied with Willie Park at Musselburgh but lost in the play-off. Andra's brother Hugh won it in 1891, the last time it was played over 36 holes. It is a source of irritation to the family that the engraved name is mis-spelt as Kirkcaldy with a 'c'. This was an error which Andra came up against frequently. His riposte was always the same. 'I'm a loon, not a toon,' he would say.

THE LONGEST SERVANT?

The Hayston club in Kirkintilloch lays claim to having had the person with the longest continuous term of office anywhere in Scotland. He is John Weir, who held various offices for 43 years before his retirement in 1989.

So long is his connection that he has seen the annual subscriptions rise almost a hundredfold from £2 2s to £210, which is not entirely his fault, even if members often playfully make it out that way.

His golfing outlook in that time has been far from parochial. On his 80th birthday in October 1988, he received greetings from Ben Crenshaw, with whom he has corresponded, Sandy Lyle, Viscount Willie Whitelaw, and Michael Bonallack and Sandy Sinclair, secretary and captain respectively, of the Royal and Ancient club.

One of his last acts as secretary was to propose Crenshaw for honorary membership, which the American has accepted and can therefore now be referred to as Ben Crenshaw (Hayston).

Among several competitions John is responsible for having introduced is the Hayston Bell, the first Sunday 36-hole event in the west of Scotland.

It is, however, the club on which bachelor John has left his biggest mark. Among his achievements are the purchase of the course and clubhouse in 1950 for £7,500, planting of the first tree on the course, building of a two-storey locker room and showers, extension of the clubhouse, installation of a steward's flat, house for the head greenkeeper, professional's shop . . . and much more.

At the retiral dinner he was showered with gifts. From the women there was an oil painting of the clubhouse and 18th green by Stephanie Graham, wife of club professional Richard, a television set and cheque from the men, and a crystal decanter from Dunbartonshire Golf Union, of which John is a past president.

There were toasts aplenty as well, which is appropriate because the 19th hole is the *raison d'être* for Hayston. At the time of founding, Kirkintilloch was a dry town and a move to install a bar at the Kirkintilloch club failed. So those who wanted a drink moved across the road and founded Hayston.

John Weir

PLAYING FOR LAUGHS

For someone who does not play golf, Craigie Veitch is fairly wowing clubhouse audiences throughout the country. After 40 years in journalism he has switched his talents from the written to the spoken word and has found laughter a regular companion.

The Silverknowes club in Edinburgh made him an honorary member and presented him with a golden key after he spoke at their prize-giving for seven years in a row, he has addressed most golf clubs in the Lothians area and his reputation is rapidly spreading west.

Members of Airdrie, Lanark and Hamilton have all risen to acclaim the Veitch-style humour and at Helensburgh — his fourth visit there — he almost brought the house down at the Brunton Miller Winter League dinner.

The former Deputy Sports Editor of the Edinburgh *Evening News* has never swung a club in anger since his boyhood days, when he travelled by tram to play Braidhills and Carrick Knowe with a borrowed set. But he talks a good game and compares golfing audiences favourably to others he has experienced.

'The people are civilised, no bread rolls are thrown, and no one is out of order,' says Veitch, whose favourite targets are Hearts chairman Wallace Mercer and former 007, Sean Connery, with whom he attended school in Edinburgh.

'Connery was much better looking than me,' intones the small, bespectacled figure, his gaunt appearance completed by a middle parting and twitching moustache. He pauses to take a sip of whisky then adds ridiculously, 'in those early days.'

Mercer, he says, laughs as much as anyone else at the barbs tossed in his direction, such as 'the only man I know who can overtake you in a revolving door' and 'when Wallace Mercer arrived in Edinburgh he possessed only a suitcase — fortunately it contained a million pounds.'

For an Edinburgh man it is surprising to hear him say he prefers audiences in the west, where the people are out simply to enjoy themselves. 'In the east I sometimes feel listeners are awarding me marks out of ten,' he says, and insists he is not a natural impromptu speaker, but has to work at it, and always has his material at the ready in an old reporter's notebook.

Veitch began speaking in his journalism days when he was sent out on behalf of his newspaper to present cups at sporting events and invariably was asked to say a few words. Since retiring 18 months ago he has been attached to the Bothwell-based agency Speakeasy and is usually heavily booked during the Burns Supper season.

'I like doing the toast to the lassies, especially if there are lassies present. So many suppers are still men-only, but on the mixed occasions I will tone things down a little and eliminate a few adjectives,' said Veitch, who admits he still gets the butterflies before standing up . . . but not so much that he cannot enjoy the meal.

'Just about everyone has had to get up and speak at some occasion, such as a wedding, and they know what an ordeal it can be. I have seen managing directors, who may have completed a million-pound deal that morning without blinking, trembling at the prospect and unable to eat.

'Because they know what it's like, they are genuinely hoping you are going to do well.'

There are two hints he passes on to occasional speakers: pause occasionally and never use the expression 'which reminds me of the story about . . .' There is, he believes, always a better way of linking items.

THE GOLF DOCTOR

Golfers in Ayrshire are more knowledgeable about technique than their cousins in the Antipodes. That statement is hardly likely to raise any eyebrows but the position put professional David Pirie to the test during a holiday back home.

David, who was an assistant at Haggs Castle and had a spell at Dumfries and County before spending six years as club professional at Brodick, is known over the airwaves in Auckland, New Zealand, as *The Golf Doctor*. Every Sunday, players telephone his radio show with their golfing ailments and he offers a cure.

He discovered, as a regular guest on Charles Currie's programme *Arran Waves* on Westsound Radio, that such a phone-in spot is also popular in Scotland.

David said: 'I found myself talking about much more advanced stuff here. There were golfers with handicaps as low as 3 phoning in and many in the 10-12 range. They were more knowledgeable about the game than in New Zealand, where I tend to concentrate on advice for beginners.

'There were not so many calls — up to six per week, about half the number in New Zealand — but the feedback was good.'

David went out to New Zealand, where he has relatives, in 1986, depressed with the Scottish weather, and found a job as teaching professional at the North Shore club, which has 27 holes and a driving range. 'If I had had a free choice, I couldn't have picked a better one,' he said.

When visiting another course, he found himself partnering a radio presenter, who invited him to the station, Newstalk IZB, as a guest. The sports presenter heard him and, thinking he spoke rather well, invited him to take up a regular hour-long Sunday evening programme.

'I usually pick one aspect of golf, such as chipping, bunker play, or driving, talk about it for a while and then open the phone lines. I also have studio guests, who have included Frank Nobilo and Greg Norman's caddie, Steve Williams.

'Golf is primarily visual, but by asking plenty of questions I can get some idea of what the problem is. I always ask callers what their handicap is, so that I know how to pitch the conversation, and then ask them to describe in detail what their fault is. I believe it works. One player even phoned in to tell me that he had reduced his handicap by 5 shots through listening in.

'But I always advise callers to visit their own club professional for a lesson to ensure they are doing things the right way.'

As with all phone-in shows you never know what is going to happen next. David was almost flummoxed when a woman phoned in to say that her problem was that she could not see the ball at address, her downward view blocked by an ample bosom.

'We cracked a few jokes about that one,' he said. 'Like not making any boobs on the course, that sort of thing. But I was able to advise her that at address she should bend from the waist and let her arms hang more freely. And because of that call we did a programme the following week entitled *Well-endowed Ladies*.'

David, who is single, plans to return to Scotland eventually, but not before enjoying the all-year-round golf in New Zealand for a few more years.

BEATING ABOUT THE BUSH

A good philosophy to have on a golf course is never to be surprised. Even in stage-managed affairs the outrageous can happen.

Take Arliss Rhind, a 19-handicapper at Letham Grange, for example. He was one of four guinea pigs selected as pupils for the latest ten-part BBC series *Play Better Golf* presented by Peter Alliss.

In one of the programmes, *Lies and Damned Lies*, in which David Huish offers advice on recovering from trouble spots, Arliss was primed to have a good thrash at a ball which had been placed in the middle of a bush.

'The idea,' he recalled, 'was to show me getting further into trouble so that viewers could be advised that the correct thing to do in such a position is to take a penalty drop.

'Anyway, I went in and had a go. The ball squirted right through the bush, down a bank and on to the green. I could hear David Huish saying: ''I have never seen anything like that in my life''.'

A video and book are available to go with the series which features lessons from John Stirling, Mickey Walker, John Jacobs, Tommy Horton, John Garner, Alex Hay, David Huish, Pip Elson and David Jones, is aimed at club golfers, and is very much in need if Alliss's view in the introduction to his book is to be taken as read.

'The carelessness of the golfer fascinates me,' he said. 'I see them arrive on the first tee wearing fashionable clothes, gloves, shoes, caps, with expensive equipment tucked into handsome golf bags.

'They haven't played for perhaps weeks, but without taking a practice swing, much less hitting a few warm-up shots on the practice ground or even into a net, they step up to the ball and make the most terrifying lunge at it.

'They've no idea about grip, stance, posture, balance or rhythm and they skull the ball almost anywhere.'

There was one aspect he didn't mention, though. Generally, in the couple of seconds it takes to hit a shot, a golfer is capable of thinking

Tommy Horton, Arliss Rhind, Peter Alliss, before

only one thought. It follows then that the best way to create confusion is to give lots of ideas all at once.

Accordingly, Arliss, along with fellow club members Neil Sharp, Cathleen Porter, and Russell Butchart, were suitably bamboozled by the finish of this devilish plot. But the evidence, with eight months'

Tommy Horton, Arliss Rhind, Peter Alliss, after

hindsight, suggests that it may not have been such a pitiless idea after all. Some are even claiming to have improved.

Neil, a chartered accountant and former club captain, was down from 25 to 24, and he identified the lesson from John Jacobs, who he regards as the best teacher in the world, as his personal highlight.

193

'Each teacher told us something slightly different and at the end we were all a little confused. I imagine the real benefit will come when we see the videos. The producer, Gordon Menzies, has already shown us some of them and when I looked at the John Jacobs one it hit me like a ton of bricks why I have been pushing the ball out to the right — that was the problem he sorted out for me and which, until I saw it again, I had forgotten about.'

Arliss, a former Fleet Street journalist who now runs two sports shops in Arbroath, agreed that the finished product is more useful than the lessons at the time, despite one golden moment on film.

He was given a day off to play in the national final of a tournament at the Belfry on condition that he was back the next morning. 'I left at 4 a.m. and just made it in time to play a two-hole match, myself and Peter Alliss against Russell and David Jones, the Irish professional. While I was half asleep I had a net eagle and a net birdie. Peter Alliss didn't get a look in.'

Cathleen, a Belfast-born mother of two, saw her handicap fall from 35 to 30 between filming and screening.

Russell, a 5-handicapper, has emigrated to America to take up a job in Minneapolis as an electrical design engineer. As a category-one player he was capable of selecting the tips useful to him. The one he remembers best came from Alex Hay. 'His advice when trying for a distance of 40 to 50 yards from a bunker was to use a No. 7 iron, open the face, and swing as if it was a fairway lie. I still use that one and have been surprised how often it works.'

All were made to feel very much at ease by the silver-tongued Alliss, who said of Arliss's amazing shot: 'Only Seve Ballesteros and the Good Lord know how that happened.'

KING TOM'S PALACE

What will become the clubhouse of the first Loch Lomond golf course, due to open in 1991, has a resemblance to that of the Royal and Ancient at St Andrews, only grander. Palatial might not be too extravagant a description, in which case, the king in residence is Tom Weiskopf.

This is the former Rossdhu House, one time home to the chiefs of the Clan Colquhoun, built a few yards from the lochside in 1773 — exactly 200 years before Weiskopf's finest day at Troon when he became Open champion — and about to become an international Mecca for swingers.

Not that Weiskopf has any airs and graces. His working clothes comprise an old cap, cardigan, working man's trousers, and a pair of Wellington boots like he would have had in his native Ohio, where he

MATCH SECRETARIES
0800 833333

Make sure your club's competition returns are in the Herald's Tuesday Club Golf page by using our FREE linkline number.

From May look out for a running tally of the best handicap and scratch scores for men and women. In the Autumn the top 10 in each section will be invited to the Herald's Parbuster tournament with six places set aside for match secretaries. There are also prizes of whisky and golf balls to be won each week.

For more informatition see the Herald's Club Golf page. Don't miss it. It's Scottish club golf's hall of fame.

Get ahead. Get the Herald.

was brought up in a farming community. He also has a personality to match.

His one concession is to remove his mud-encrusted wellies before stretching out on a settee in the large, wood-panelled drawing-room to expound on his latest venture — on behalf of UK developer David Brench — of which he says: 'It is going to be world renowned; I know it will be. There is no prettier place in the world in my eyes.'

The clubhouse, which is being renovated and extended at a cost of more than £3m, and the 6,845-yard course (The High Road) co-designed by his partner Jay Morrish, on which fractionally less is being invested, will be the pride and joy of a £40m development by Stirling Investments which will include a second course (The Low Road), a 200-bedroom hotel, and a 200-berth marina.

Of the parkland course accessed off the A82 just short of Luss, 46-year-old Weiskopf, already the designer of 15 courses in America, says: 'It will not be American-style, although it will have watered fairways. However, it is being designed by two Americans, and will have our personalities. There are four holes where the loch will come into play, a pond at another, and two streams, but we will not be creating anything in the way of water hazards which are not here already.

'We are trying to beautify and clean up the banks, will be planting flowering shrubs, daffodils, tulips, and bluebells, and redistributing some rhododendrons. Whatever is native to the countryside we will plant in areas we think need to be beautified, and Dave (Brench) has done a pretty rock wall in the same style as ones built hundreds of years ago to prevent erosion.

'It will be dramatic and aesthetically very beautiful. There will be three or four tees on each hole so players will be able to pick their own poison and choose a test to match their abilities. It will be extremely challenging but fair, and will have the basic characteristic of golf in Scotland in that you will be able to bounce the ball on to the green. The approach to all greens will be open.

'There will be no controversial holes — Jay and I do not deal in that — but there will be a different challenge to each hole. It will, I hope, favour accurate rather than long hitters, and there are as many holes playing to the left as there are to the right so that it will favour neither hooker nor fader.

'We are also trying to design some subtle mounding so that if we have a big tournament, there will be vantage points, and I believe the practice area will prove to be the best in the British Isles. It will be 325 yards long and double-ended, allowing players to practise from both ends, 100 yards wide with three or four greens, several bunkers, and depressed in the middle so that you are looking down at your target.'

Tom Weiskopf

It all sounds quite magnificent and there is a price to match — £25,000 (corporate membership for four) for a five-year period, and an overseas price of £10,000 for a lifetime, with a total of 400 members. There are plans for a limited individual membership when the second course opens and visitors will be restricted to members' guests.

Weiskopf, wife Jeanne, son Eric, and daughter Heidi, will be making regular visits, and he feels very much at home in Scotland.

'I think Scots people are the greatest, a lot more friendly in general than the English, and much more down to earth. Scots golfers are traditionalists and the game for many is very much a way of life. It is good to see, and I would like to do something special for them,' said Weiskopf, who has shown himself to be just as comfortable with royalty as he is with ordinary folk, as witness one of his favourite stories which happened at Muirfield during the 1972 Open.

All seats in the clubhouse were taken, so he pulled a cushion off a chair and sat down on the floor next to a woman, a complete stranger, with whom he struck up a conversation. After a while she got up — and so did almost everyone else — and left. 'Do you know who you were speaking to?' he was asked. 'For all I know it could have been the Queen,' he replied.

In fact, it was Princess Margaret to whom Tom later apologised for his lack of protocol and asked: 'Do you play golf?' 'No,' replied the princess, 'but my father did.' Whereupon he asked: 'And what did he do for a living?'

'He was the king,' said the princess matter-of-factly.

It won't be long before Tom Weiskopf has his own place on Loch Lomond which is fit for one.

197

THE EQUALISING
FACTORS

Golf handicaps have always been a source of controversy. They put a gloss on sometimes appalling scores. A club golfer might tell you: 'I went round in 68 — 4 under par.' A tremendous player, you might think. What he will probably omit to tell you is that his handicap is 22, a figure which was deducted from his score. In fact, he went round in a somewhat less impressive 90.

Surely no device can cause more arguments than this one. A 7-handicapper who went round in 76 (net 69) and was pipped by one despite having taken 14 fewer shots might have grounds for feeling hard done by.

Yet the handicap system is amateur golf's greatest strength. It enables players of all abilities to compete against each other on an equal footing. At least that is the ultimate objective. Equality is often elusive in golf, and the variable standard scratch score scheme is the latest attempt to achieve this.

For those unfamiliar with golfing parameters, the par of a hole, determined for men by length, is usually 3, 4 or 5 — the number of strokes a golfer would be expected to take without either making a mistake or doing anything brilliant.

The par of the course is the sum of these 18 figures which is usually close to or the same as the standard scratch score, which is determined by the overall length of the course. For example, if there are a lot of short par 4s, the course may be par 69, SSS 67, and with many long par 4s, it could be par 69, SSS 71.

Previously no account was taken of conditions. Obviously scoring on a cold, windy day will not be as good as on a calm, sunny day. The variable scratch score scheme which, when computed, becomes the competition scratch score (CSS) will reflect conditions by determining the base score according to the performance of players in any one competition. It works like this:

The percentage of scores two over SSS or better are set up against the total entry in three groups according to handicap, the lowest handicap group weighted to give it the greatest effect on the grounds that the performance of good players is a better guide. The result will vary the SSS by a maximum of 3 more or 1 less. If the scores are so bad that they do not come within the limits of the plus 3 banding then the competition will be declared a non-counter.

A clear advantage is that the system will eliminate the personal views of club handicap-conveners in deciding non-counting days. There have been cases in the past of different clubs using the same course on the same day, one declaring the competition a non-counter and the other a counter. A disadvantage is that a competitor will not know how his handicap has altered until every competitor is finished.

The system was designed by the Council of National Golf Unions (CONGU) with the advice of statistics experts and is likely to undergo further modifications with the introduction of course rating, the setting of SSS in relation to severity of hazards as well as course length. At the time of writing no timescale had been set for its introduction.

A new definition of the term 'bandit' soon became necessary in the light of the statistics that follow, a pattern which had already been suspected as a result of speaking to the bandits involved. In the first instance, way back in May 1988, we described a bandit as a reasonably good player with a high handicap. In the context used herein, a bandit can be re-defined as a genuine player who has just enjoyed his or her round of a lifetime.

An estimate of the field represented by our returns in peak summer is 10,000 golfers. An individual would have to play four rounds of golf a week over a period of almost 50 years to tally this number of rounds. Hence, topping Parbusters — our weekly listing of the nation's leading bandits — has to be, statistically, a once-in-a-lifetime experience.

Confirmation came from Bill Mitchell of Johnstone, who, for the second year running, has analysed an entire season's club returns from the *Herald*. Bill asked whether these players, the 'cream of the bandits', are a breed to be despised or an acceptable part of the golfing race. His analysis showed that the handicap breakdown of 430 parbusters by percentage was:

Category 1 (5 or less) 7
Category 2 (6-12) 23
Category 3 (13-20) 45
Category 4 (21-28) 25

This, said Bill, is a fairly typical split of competitors in any club competition, and 'leads to the conclusion that the Parbusters are not a race apart and the fond thought that on a good day any one of us could join this select band'.

He also analyses whether the present handicapping system is fair to all classes of golfers. Almost 1,500 returns were examined, treating all competitions as open to all classes and looking only at clubs with an upper limit of 28 (those operating limits of 18-24 were excluded).

The breakdown by percentage of winning scores, with comparisons to 1988, is:

	1989	1988
Category 1 (5 or less)	7	7
Category 2 (6-12)	32	34
Category 3 (13-20)	43	37
Category 4 (21-28)	18	22

This again shows a similar breakdown to that which would be expected of an average club entry. The conclusion, therefore, is that the variable standard scratch system is equitable.

Bill, furthermore, examined the scoring required to win a medal in the various classes, and how this compared with conditions as reflected by the competition scratch score. The outcome, with figures for 1988 in brackets, was:

	STROKES BELOW SSS		
CSS	1st Class	2nd Class	3rd Class
−1	5.5(5.5)	6.0(6.0)	6.0(5.5)
0	4.0(4.0)	4.5(4.5)	4.0(4.0)
+1	2.5(2.5)	3.0(3.0)	2.5(2.0)
+2	1.5(1.5)	1.5(2.0)	1.5(1.0)
+3	1	0	0

Bill concluded that results show good agreement across handicap classes, a sensible correlation with conditions, and consistency in that the level of scoring required is remarkably similar in both 1988 and 1989 — further proof that the system is equitable.

Frequency of change in the standard scratch score and how this related to course conditions resulted, with figures expressed in percentages and those of 1988 in brackets, as follows:

MONTH	VARIATION IN SSS				
	−1	+0	+1	+2	+3
April	0	15	23	31	31
May	3(1)	58(55)	22(25)	13(13)	4(6)
June	13(11)	73(71)	10(13)	4(5)	0(0)

MONTH	VARIATION IN SSS				
	− 1	+ 0	+ 1	+ 2	+ 3
July	30(19)	61(71)	7(9)	2(1)	0(0)
August	32(8)	53(77)	7(11)	5(3)	3(1)
September	3(0)	71(48)	18(27)	6(17)	2(11)

Bill also found these figures reasonable. The big increases in April and May can be explained, he said, by poor greens and rusty swings, the good weather of the summer of 1989 responsible for more drops in the SSS than the year before, and the 'normal' wind and rain of September causing more rises again.

We are extremely grateful for this analysis and all the painstaking work that went into it. The overall conclusion has to be that whether or not we understand how our handicapping system works, we should accept that it does and question it no further.

The system did, however, throw up one peculiar instance, and it was with no sense of history in the making that Ken Greig, a retired doctor, began his round in the usual blustery conditions at Western Gailes in a midweek medal. Neither did he imagine some three hours later that his round of 94, a net 73 and 1 over the standard scratch score, would go down in the annals of the club.

Only when you look at this respectable if rather unspectacular return against the performance of all other competitors does its significance jump out of the scorecard and bite you on the nose. You see, there were only two entrants.

The other was 22-handicapper John Wright, Dr Greig's playing partner, who deemed his card unworthy of return.

It does not need membership of Mensa to work out in the current handicap jargon that 50 per cent of the field were in the buffer zone (1 or 2 over par). Just to make sure, however, the club ran the details through their computer, which duly came up with the unprecedented calculation that the competition scratch score was 1 less than the SSS.

Since the variable SSS scheme was introduced, Western Gailes has proved itself a tougher course than its basic rating. Only twice has the SSS remained at 72. On all other occasions it has gone up, usually by more than 1. With a full entry, Dr Greig would likely have had his handicap cut. Never before had it dropped to 71.

The club's midweek medals, one-off competitions which qualify the winner for nothing other than the glory and the lion's share of the sweep, attract up to 30 competitors on summer evenings. Restricted daylight in winter means fewer are able to play, although two is an all-time low.

The sting in the tail is that neither player entered the sweep, and so Dr Greig was denied even a measly 50p. But history is priceless!

Another modification, which is slowly catching on, is that a player's exact handicap — the system deals in decimal points and a player's handicap is usually rounded up or down — is used instead of the more common better inward half to decide ties. Fereneze and Kilmarnock Barassie are two such clubs.

There is, of course, more than one way of skinning a cat, and the women have their own method of calculating handicap. There are five categories, A to E. Group E comprises those with handicaps of between 30 and 36, whose mark is determined by the difference between the player's best score and the scratch score of the course. Category D, handicap range 19-29, is fixed by the average of the two best scores, C (10-18) by the average of the four best scores, B (4-9) by the average of the six best scores. Category A (3 and under) requires the average of ten best scores, four of which must be from two courses other than a player's home course.

The men's and women's methods are vastly different in operation, but there is a view that the net effect of both is not far apart.

THE BMW SYNDROME

Golf professionals are not just good at striking balls. They have to be good at business as well and are becoming ever more sophisticated. They are trained to be public-relations conscious and to be capable of surviving in the hi-tech world of finance as well as being craftsmen and coaches. The approaches of club committees are changing as well, but while more and more are forward looking there remains a stuffy attitude among some, which the Scottish Professional Golfers' Association is doing its level best to kill.

The danger is that with the European golf boom, newly-qualified professionals are being attracted abroad by the prospect of salaries often three times the level they would earn in Scotland — and without the overheads of running a sometimes woefully inadequate shop. Green-keepers are in the same position, and these topics have regularly cropped up over the last two years. The following scene may be familiar.

The regular weekend four are sitting with their beers in the corner of the club bar after their round. 'Have you seen the expensive new car our professional is driving?' asks one. 'Yes, ridiculous, isn't it,' comes the reply. 'It's members like us that keep him in a job. Living in the lap of luxury he is. Nice house, best of clothes. We pay the rent for his shop, and he wants an increase I hear. There's no way I'm voting for that. A reduction would be more like it.'

It is described as 'the BMW syndrome' by Sandy Jones, secretary of the Scottish region of the Professional Golfers' Association, and it is one which, in most cases, he says, is totally unjustified.

He knows of instances where club professionals have been forced to own two cars. There is the good one which is kept at home, well under wraps, and the inoffensive banger which is driven to the club and which the members can see and approve of. The flash-car image is a definite no-no.

'It's a peculiar Scottish attitude,' says Jones. 'If the professional does not appear to be doing well, the club will encourage him, suggest that he smartens up, and take an interest in his progress. But if he is too successful, some members are liable to turn against him. Why shouldn't they be proud if their man has made it to the top?

'If it was America they would love it, but we like to build people up and then knock them down, and it is true in all walks of life, not just golf. Look at Ally MacLeod at the World Cup in Argentina. I could hardly believe the tumble he took in the space of just a few weeks.'

Crusty club-committee attitudes sometimes extend to misplaced feelings of superior status, such as the case in which Jones was asked along to an east of Scotland club to discuss the professional's payment.

'The captain told me at the meeting that there was no way he could authorise a rise because if he did, then the professional would be earning more than he did,' he said. 'What's that got to do with it? The club is his hobby, but it is the professional's livelihood, and as an employer, he has to make sure he is well looked after.'

It does not necessarily follow that because a professional drives a big car, his business is healthy, says Jones. 'It may be that he needs a comfortable car because of the high mileage he puts in to work off a large overdraft. In many cases, club officials tell me their professional is doing well without having any detailed knowledge of whether he is or is not. This is not the case at all clubs, but it is a very common attitude.'

The average retainer in 1990 paid to Scotland's 150 club professionals was between £3,500 and £4,000, and Jones reckons that evaluated realistically, the service to the club, net of free rent for the shop, is between £8,000 and £9,000, the kind of sum a growing number of clubs are paying.

'For that retainer and provision of a shop, the club will expect a service 12 hours a day, seven days a week, 364 days a year. How many businesses stay open that long?' asks Jones. 'Just 364 days?' 'Yes they usually get either Christmas or New Year's Day off, but not both.'

The minimum payment for Scotland's 100 assistants was £42 a week in 1990 — barely enough for a person to live on. But even subsistence wages like that tend to use up more than half the professional's retainer.

What Jones would like to see eventually is a grading system for clubs, one of the criteria being a sliding scale of minimum payments. Already there are the beginnings of this in that club facilities are vetted by the PGA and must be passed as up to standard before they will allow an assistant to be appointed.

He reckons a full grading system is several years away. Who knows, by that time it may be compulsory for a grade-one club to have a parking space for the professional's Rolls-Royce.

Once the smart car is parked, the problems do not end. The professional may then enter his workplace which is akin to a 'converted telephone box', according to David Huish, professional at North Berwick and a former captain of the British PGA.

'In many cases professionals are expected to work out of a very small area even although their job has changed so much over the years. It used to be that a professional would stock a few balls, clubs, and shoes, but the style of the golfer has also undergone a big change.

'Golfers used to arrive at the club wearing their good gear and change into old clothes to play. Now it is almost the opposite. They like to dress up in the latest fashions before going out on the course.'

Huish, who travels widely in Scotland, said he has been dismayed in many cases to see shops far too small for the proper display of a burgeoning range of patterned sweaters, shirts, and shoes. 'They never look quite so attractive when they are stacked in poly bags — the customer cannot see them properly. Frequently, the professional is reduced to keeping his stock either in his house, up in the loft, or somewhere in the back shop far away from customers.'

It is not just the department-store aspect that is lacking. Shops are increasingly becoming a focal point for members to book tee-off times and enter competitions, and for visitors to pay green fees and collect scorecards. It is an all-too-familiar occurrence for players to be tripping over each other on a Saturday morning.

Professionals also need a workshop, big enough so that they are not operating on top of their stock of equipment, and an office area as well, preferably with a door which can be closed when peace and quiet is required for an increasing amount of bookwork.

'I don't want to mention the bad ones — but there are an awful lot,' said Huish. 'I am lucky here at North Berwick, and when golfers visit courses like Gleneagles, Turnberry, and Gullane they see a nice display and wonder why they cannot have the same at their own club.

'What I would like to see happen whenever opportunities arise, is for good-sized shops to be incorporated into designs. There is a tendency for clubs to build extensions for reasons like changing rooms for visitors and then wonder where they are going to put the professional.

'The same kind of thing also happens too often in the design of courses. The holes are laid out and then people wonder where they are going to put the practice ground which should have been part of the design in the first place.'

One place this kind of scheme did happen was at Paisley, where a new shop was designed within a clubhouse extension ready for Grant

Gilmour to become the first modern-style professional at the club, which is known as The Bushes.

Grant, previously an assistant at Hilton Park and before that at Cowal, was, in early 1990, the 165th Scottish club professional, a fact unearthed by Sandy Jones when he checked the statistics to mark his 10 years with the PGA. In 1980 there were just 122 club professionals. If you work it out that means there has been one new job every 85 days since 1980, a rate of job creation of which Margaret Thatcher would be proud.

'I was astonished at the figures — it was a far bigger increase than I had thought,' said Sandy. 'But clubs are much busier now than they were ten years ago. There are more people playing the sport and you cannot ask a club steward to act as starter and attend to all the needs of visitors. More and more clubs are turning to a professional.' Among those clubs who had taken on a professional since 1980 are Fereneze, Lenzie, Kirriemuir, Canmore, Caldwell, Brodick, Dumfries and Galloway, Westhill, Montrose, Lochwinnoch, and Ranfurly Castle. More could well be on the way, but said Sandy, there is a limit. 'There are a number of nine-hole courses which will never require a professional, but I can see such clubs getting together and taking on one professional to look after various outlets where perhaps an assistant might be in charge.'

The road abroad is often more attractive, and with the game undergoing a tremendous boom in Europe comparisons are already being drawn with the state of the game in America at the turn of the century, when leading Scottish professionals made the trans-Atlantic trip — and look what happened there!

Early in 1989 Hugh Cairns of Royal Troon was one Scottish assistant to opt for the continental route to fame and fortune. The 25-year-old was moving to take up the head teaching professional's job at the Homburger Club, near Frankfurt. 'The game is really taking off in Europe, where golfers cannot seem to get enough lessons. Because there are still comparatively few golf courses, members are generally wealthy and do not mind paying well for equipment and tuition. I will be able to earn three times as much there and also have free accommodation.'

The general affluence of that area is such that members are paying annual subscriptions of around £3,000 a year, and speak English. Although golf language is fast becoming universal, Hugh was taking a course in German to help him along the way.

Later in the year Stephen Skinner, trained at Lanark, and Iain Gold, a product of Hollandbush, headed for the land of the midnight sun fresh after passing their PGA examinations. Stephen was taking up a summer job at the Skellaftea club, 130 miles from the Arctic Circle, and claimed to be the most northerly 18-hole course in the world, while Iain was taking up a similar post at Umea, 60 miles further south.

Greenkeepers, too, are looking to improvements in training, and expressing concern that the best are lured abroad because rewards in Scotland are often pitiful. Chris Kennedy, the course manager at Haggs Castle until early in 1990 when he took up the head greenkeeper's job at Wentworth, feels strongly that improvements must be made to attract and to keep the right people.

Chris's views were expressed shortly after the discussion document, *The Way Forward*, which criticised standards of British greenkeeping, had just been released by the R and A, who were to help fund improvements. One point made is a need for further education for greenkeepers — a subject close to his heart as a former Scottish Region Administrator of the British and International Golf Greenkeepers' Association. 'We are leading from the front,' said Chris, who believes that Scotland is a decade ahead of England in terms of educating greens staff, qualifications having been introduced in 1966 and students receiving tuition in horticulture, mechanics, biology, chemistry, and mathematics.

Courses for greens staff are already in place at five Scottish colleges — Elmwood (Cupar), Langside (Glasgow), Ayr Technical, Dundee Technical, and Oatridge (Edinburgh). His association, along with delegates from colleges and the Scottish Golf Union, forms the Scottish Greenkeepers' Training Committee, which draws up curricula.

The R and A document also urges firmer, faster, and truer greens, and mud free fairways, aspects which he regards as sound but difficult to put into practice because of individuality of courses and budget limitations.

However, further education of club greens conveners is a recommendation with which he disagrees, not least because of the lack of continuity for 'well-meaning amateurs put in a terrible position for a period of one to three years'. Frequently volunteers, they are not spared — even by their friends — if the course is in a poor condition. Chris adds: 'Then, by the time a good working relationship is established with the greens staff, their period of office is over and it is someone else's turn. Private clubs are not businesses, they are run for members, which is good in some ways — but the management committee does change. I would rather see the role of greens convener become one of liaison between the permanent greens staff, who are responsible for the condition of the course, and the committee.'

What all this adds up to is a clear indication that clubs are going to have to pay more, if they want to keep pace with improvements in personnel, course and clubhouse facilities. The days of cheap golf could soon be over.

A GRACE FOR CARRADALE GOLF CLUB

God our Father,
We thank you that playing over our course
We see part of the beauty of your creation
We thank you for friendship
And healthy competition.

Bless our gathering this evening
And accept our gratitude for your gifts set before us.

Grant, O Lord, that throughout our lives
We may strive to stay on your fairway
Enable us to cope with the awkward lie
And the bad bounce
Give us strength and perseverance in the rough places.

Keep us from going out of bounds
So that when the round of life is complete
We may enter your Clubhouse
With its many rooms.

Alistair J Dunlop,
Carradale 1988

The Rev. Dunlop, minister of Saddell and Carradale Parish Church, writer of this grace has observed: 'After its first use there was a round of applause. 'Amen' might have been more appropriate.'